Face to Face

A Primer in Dialogue

∽ℰℊ

A Jewish Heritage Book
Edited by Lily Edelman

Published by
B'nai B'rith Adult Jewish Education
Anti-Defamation League of B'nai B'rith
Crown Publishers Inc.

ACKNOWLEDGMENTS:

"What Ecumenism Is" from *The Insecurity of Freedom* by Abraham
J. Heschel (Farrar, Straus & Giroux, Inc., 1966)
Answers to questions found in "Questions Christians Ask" adapted
from *Basic Judaism* by Milton Steinberg (Harcourt Brace, 1947)

Jewish Heritage Editorial Office
1640 Rhode Island Ave., N.W.
Washington, D. C. 20036

Table of Contents

Introduction

Yesterday: Auschwitz. And today a new day in Jewish-Christian rapprochement. Out of the ashes of the six million — whose sole crime was being Jewish — there rises, in the hearts of sincere, responsible Christians everywhere, a yearning to understand, a need to know, a desire to turn from the bloodletting of the past to a guilt-free future.

"A deep sense of shame" must haunt Christians, affirms Father H. J. Richards, a British educator, after a pilgrimage to Yad Vashem, Jerusalem's stark holocaust memorial. "You are struck numb with shame that this should have been done by our own contemporaries, while we looked the other way . . . that this should have been defended (as it was) in the name of Christianity, as if our Christian Faith somehow demanded that this is how we should treat the Jews. . ."

Nor is this the first instance of brutality inflicted on Jews as Jews, Father Richards confesses. "It has been going on in waves throughout the history of Christendom. Since Europe became Christian there has scarcely been a time in which, in one country or another, Jews have not been abused, slandered, plundered, deported, enslaved, tortured and put to death."*

In a massive outburst of Christian conscience, the impact of which cannot yet be fully measured or predicted, opportunities for dialogue between Jews and Christians are proliferating at a rate which even a year ago would have seemed impossible if not Messianic. Religious texts are being revised, courses on Judaism introduced in Christian seminaries, joint Judeo-Christian scholarly ventures in Bible study initiated. In Madrid, the scene of so much historic Jewish suffering, Jews and Catholics are led in common prayer and psalm by priest and cantor. In Holland the Dutch Reformed Church announces an end to its traditional "mission to the Jews," long a sore point in Jewish-Christian relations. In the United States, the National Conference of Catholic Bishops issues a set of highly specific guidelines for new bonds of understanding and dialogue on all levels with Jews and Judaism.

As the Jericho walls which so long separated Jews from their Christian neighbors come tumbling down, the crucial question

---

* In the Anglo-Catholic quarterly (published in Paris), *Encounter Today: Judaism and Christianity in the Contemporary World*, Vol. I, No. 1, Winter-Spring 1966; formerly *The Jews and Ourselves*.

for Jews is: are we ready? Now that the doors of ecumenism are swinging wide open, are we prepared for meaningful confrontation with Christians?

No: in truth, we are neither ready nor prepared. "There aren't enough Jews to go around" is Arthur Gilbert's blunt assessment. Quoted in a recent front-page article in the *New York Times** devoted to the new accelerated opportunities for "dialogue among the three faiths," Rabbi Gilbert refers of course to the lack of literate Jewish laymen familiar and at home with matters of Jewish practice and belief, in whose hands the success or failure of such encounter ultimately rests.

What dialogue requires is self-knowledge and commitment on the part of Jewish participants: this is the theme and the thrust of this special, enlarged issue of *Jewish Heritage,* published in cooperation with the Anti-Defamation League of B'nai B'rith. "It is bad enough when a Jew is fuzzy about his own heritage among his own people," warns Israel Mowshowitz. But "it is disastrous for him to enter into dialogue with others without a solid basis and background of Judaism." Jay Kaufman is even more emphatic in insisting that knowledge and "bona fide credentials" are prerequisities for dialogue. "The presence of inadequately prepared Jewish laymen purporting to speak as their people's representatives is a spiritual fraud," he affirms.

The material presented here is an attempt to provide the beginnings of the Jewish knowledge that is required. Dealing with aspects of the ongoing Jewish-Christian dialogue from a variety of vantage points, some articles analyze what dialogue is and what it is not, its potentials, its limitations. A second group of pieces—the largest—are devoted to interpreting specific matters of belief which have long been subjects of Christian-Jewish difference: e.g., Jesus and the crucifixion, the Chosen People concept, the Old and New Covenants. A third cluster discusses and interprets Vatican Council II and its Schema, providing in itself an interreligious dialogue on this crucial, far-reaching document.

No attempt has been made to be all-inclusive or representative of all views on dialogue within either the Christian or Jewish communities. Our aim is more modest: to provide readers with the desire—and some introductory materials—to ready themselves for the "great day" a-coming: Jewish-Christian understanding rooted in mutual self-knowledge and self-respect. Only then can all God's children consecrate themselves to the task of remaining human in a world not of our own making.   —Lily Edelman

* February 20, 1967.

What Ecumenism Is

Abraham J. Heschel

When Israel approached Sinai, God lifted up the mountain and held it over their heads, saying: "Either you accept the Torah or be crushed beneath the mountain."

The mountain of history is over our heads again. Shall we renew the covenant with God?

In the words of Isaiah: "The envoys of peace weep bitterly. . . . Covenants are broken, witnesses are despised, there is no regard for man" (33:7-8).

Men all over the world have a dreadful sense in common, the fear of absolute evil, the fear of total annihilation. An apocalyptic monster has descended upon the world, and there is nowhere to go, nowhere to hide.

This is an hour when even men of reason call for accommodation to absolute evil and preparation for disaster, maintaining that certain international problems are weird, demonic, beyond solution.

Dark is the world for us, for all its cities and stars. If not for Thee, O Lord, who could stand such anguish, such disgrace?

The gap between the words we preach and the lives we live threatens to become an abyss. How long will we tolerate a situation that refutes what we confess?

Is it not true that God and nuclear stockpiles cannot dwell together in one world? Is it not true that facing disaster together we must all unite to defy despair, to prevent surrender to the demonic?

The minds are sick. The hearts are mad. Humanity is drunk with a sense of absolute sovereignty. Our pride is hurt by each other's arrogance.

The dreadful predicament is not due to economic conflicts. It is due to a spiritual paralysis.

This is an age of suspicion, when most of us seem to live by the rule: Suspect thy neighbor as thyself. Such radical suspicion leads to despair of man's capacity to be free and to eventual surrender to demonic forces, surrender to idols of power, to the monsters of self-righteous ideologies.

What will save us is a revival of reverence for man, unmitigable indignation at acts of violence, burning compassion for all who are deprived, the wisdom of the heart. Before imputing guilt to others, let us examine our own failures.

What all men have in common is poverty, anguish, insecurity. What all religions have in common is power to refute the fallacy of absolute expediency, insistence that the dignity of man is in his power of compassion, in his capacity for sacrifice, self-denial.

Our era marks the end of complacency. We all face the dilemma expressed by Moses: "I have put before you life and death, blessing and curse. Choose life." Religion's task is to cultivate disgust for violence and lies, sensitivity to other people's suffering, the love of peace. God has a stake in the life of every man. He never exposes humanity to a challenge without giving humanity the power to face the challenge.

Different are the languages of prayer, but the tears are the same. We have a vision in common of Him in whose compassion all men's prayers meet.

In the words of the prophet Malachi, "From the rising of the sun to its setting My name is great among the nations, in every place incense is offered to My name, and a pure offering; for My name is great among the nations, says the Lord of hosts" (Malachi: 1:11). It seems to me that the prophet proclaims that men all over the world, though they confess different conceptions of God, are really worshipping One God, the Father of all men, though they may not even be aware of it.

What will save us? God, and our faith in man's relevance to God.

This is the agony of history: bigotry, the failure to respect each other's commitment, each other's faith. We must insist upon loyalty to the unique and holy treasures of our own tradition and at the same time acknowledge that in this aeon religious diversity may be the providence of God.

Respect for each other's commitment, respect for each other's faith, is more than a political and social imperative. It is born of the insight that God is greater than religion, that faith is deeper than dogma, that theology has its roots in depth theology.

The ecumenical perspective is the realization that religious truth does not shine in a vacuum, that the primary issue of theology is pretheological, and that religion involves the total situation of man, his attitudes and deeds, and must therefore never be kept in isolation.

It is customary to blame secular science and antireligious philosophy for the eclipse of religion in modern society. It would be more honest to blame religion for its own defeats. Religion declined not because it was refuted, but because it became irrelevant, dull, oppressive, insipid. When faith is completely replaced by creed, worship by discipline, love by habit; when the crisis of today is ignored because of the splendor of the past; when faith becomes an heirloom rather than a living fountain; when religion speaks only in the name of authority rather than with the voice of compassion—its message becomes meaningless.

The great spiritual renewal within the Roman Catholic Church, inspired by Pope John XXIII, is a manifestation of the dimension of depth of religious existence. It already has opened many hearts and unlocked many precious insights.

There is a longing for peace in the hearts of man. But peace is not the same as the absence of war. Peace among men depends upon a relationship of reverence for each other.

Reverence for man means reverence for man's freedom. God has a stake in the life of man, of every man.

It was in the spirit of depth theology that Cardinal Bea announced his intention to prepare a constitution on religious liberty for presentation at the (Vatican) Council, in which the Fathers would be asked to come out emphatically with a public recognition of the inviolability of the human conscience as the final right of every man, no matter what his religious beliefs or ideological allegiance. Cardinal Bea stated further that the axiom "Error has no right to exist," which is used so glibly by certain Catholic apologists, is sheer nonsense, for error is an abstract concept incapable of either rights or obligations. It is persons who have rights, and even when they are in error, their right to freedom of conscience is absolute.

To quote from classic rabbinic literature: "Pious men of all nations have a share in the world to come," and are promised the reward of eternal life. "I call heaven and earth to witness that the Holy Spirit rests upon each person, Jew or Gentile, man or woman, master or slave, in consonance with his deeds."

God's voice speaks in many languages, communicating itself in a diversity of intuitions.

The word of God never comes to an end. No word is God's last word.

Man's greatest task is to comprehend God's respect and regard for the freedom of man, freedom, the supreme manifestation of God's regard for man.

In the words of Pope John's Encyclical, *Pacem in Terris:* "Every human being has the right to freedom in searching for truth and in expressing and communicating his opinions. . . . Every human being has the right to honor God according to the dictates of an upright conscience."

Man's most precious thought is God, but God's most precious thought is man.

A religious man is a person who holds God and man in one thought at one time, at all times, who suffers in himself harms done to others, whose greatest passion is compassion, whose greatest strength is love and defiance of despair.

If I Were Christian

If I were Christian, I would try to help the Jew to be as Jewish as I the Christian would wish to be Christian. I would say to the Jew: Be Jewish, gloriously, positively, affirmatively, wholesomely Jewish. For this society we must together build, lest paganism and brutality drive out all decency, and God become the greatest refugee of all, we want of you, the Jew, not alone your brawn and the sweat of your brow, but also the distilled wisdom of the centuries, the precious insights of your history, and accumulated riches of your experience, the understanding and tenderness born of your suffering. Give your whole self, as I would give my whole self, so that on the firm Gibraltar of brotherhood we may together build the good life, the city of God, the Kingdom of Heaven.

Rabbi Morris Adler,
May I Have a Word With You?
(Crown, 1967)

Why Dialogue?

Israel Mowshowitz

A very thoughtful Christian must confront the challenge of Auschwitz.

The holocaust did not take place in some isolated, barren corner of the earth. The drama of the greatest slaughter in the history of mankind was enacted in the very middle of Christian Europe, staged by "Christian" Germany, with the cooperation and collaboration of Polish, Ukrainian and other Christians. Honest and painful soul-searching has brought Christians face to face with the terrible truth that anti-Semitism has its Christian roots. What happened to Jews in the Nazi era may have been due in no inconsiderable measure to the centuries long process of "the teaching of contempt" by the Church about Jews and Judaism. A sense of guilt and shame has led many in the Christian world, if not to repentance, at least to *hirhurei t'shuva,* to intimations of repentance, to a desire to re-evaluate historic Christian-Jewish relations.

Reflecting this new attitude is the declaration of the Lutheran World Federation in Denmark in April, 1964.

> "Christian" anti-Semitism is spiritual suicide. This phenomenon presents a unique question to the Christian Church, especially in light of the long and terrible history of Christian culpability to anti-Semitism. No Christian can exempt himself from involvement in this guilt. As Lutherans, we confess our own peculiar guilt, and we lament with shame the responsibility which our church and her people bear for this sin. We can only ask God's pardon and that of the Jewish people . . .

Protestant and Catholic educators are today making careful studies of textbooks used in their religious schools in order to remove objectionable material that may lend itself to anti-Semitic interpretations. Many church groups have extended a call to Jews to enter into dialogue with them out of a desire for authentic information. Until now they knew them only in caricature, as a prop for their own doctrinal needs. The Jew was accepted and studied not as a person with a faith commitment of his own, but as a witness to the truth of classical Christian theology.

A New Day

The call for dialogue is an expression of the dawning realization on the part of many Christians that Judaism is not petrified history, but a living faith which has something to contribute to our times. Father John B. Sheerin, editor of *The Catholic World*, made this quite clear with the following comment about the Vatican Council statement on the Jews:

> Dialogue must be built on mutual respect, but many Jews feel that the Jewish statement shows respect for the prophets and the religion of ancient Israel but not for the religion of modern Jews. If this were true, the Council would be saying in effect that the only good Jews are dead Jews. This was certainly not the mind of the Council, for it said in the Jewish declaration that the Church cannot forget that "she draws sustenance from the root of that well-cultivated olive tree unto which have been grafted the wild shoots, the Gentiles.". . .
>
> The Jews then still have a special divine call, and we should show reverence for the living religion of the Jews by acknowledging it as a valid and authentic supernatural reality.

Now that we are no more looked upon as a meta-theological construct but rather as a flesh-and-blood reality, communication between Jews and Christians becomes both possible and necessary.

In *The King's Persons*, Joanne Greenberg relates the story of the destruction of the Jewish community of York in the twelfth century. She writes of the surreptitious friendship that developed between Abram, a young Jew, and the Catholic Brother Simon. On one occasion the young monk pleads earnestly with his young Jewish friend, "Can you not try to dissuade your leaders from their taste for blood of Christians in their rituals?" The author describes Abram's reaction:

> Indignation and laughter seemed to stand side by side in Abram as he spoke to Brother Simon, yet he felt somehow that this Brother was not closed against his words, not frightened of him or of his honesty.
>
> He told Simon of the wine, not blood, which blessed all holy meals and feasts, and he spoke of the abhorrence of Jews for the unclean. As he did he felt the monk drinking in his words. He grew expansive and large of gesture, enjoying the proofs as they came to him, amplifying the points of his explanation almost joyfully.
>
> He felt wonderfully free.
>
> When he was finished, Brother Simon looked for a long time at him, his eyes opened very wide with seeing all that was new to him. Then he said slowly, "I never knew such things. Have we been alive together in the same world?"

Christians and Jews, we are alive together in the same world. It is therefore important that we make an honest effort to understand one another. It may be easier, but certainly not better, for Jews and Christians to live in their respective self-imposed theological and spiritual ghettos. Lack of communication between authoritative representatives of both faith communities will lead to the worst type of ignorance, that described by a famous humorist as "knowin' so many things that ain't so."

An important sociological factor also lies behind the call by many Christians for dialogue with the Jewish community. Religion in our times faces the challenge of the forces of materialism and secularism which lay claim to an exclusive concern with, and commitment to, the welfare of man. Religion has been accused of conducting a cloistered existence, far removed from the arena of life. It has been suggested that religion has been trying to answer questions that nobody asks. The danger to religion is that it may be dismissed as irrelevant. Christians and Jews must therefore work together to strengthen the spiritual concept of man and society. They must show a greater social concern and pool their strength toward the building of a more equitable social order. Our respective spiritual imperatives should lead us to a partnership in many areas of the quest for the betterment of the human lot.

Opposition to Dialogue

Where few in the Jewish community would oppose dialogue in the field of social action, there are many voices raised in warning against entering into dialogue involving religious commitment.

Why a Christian-Jewish dialogue, one writer asks, why not a Hindu-Jewish dialogue, or Buddhist-Jewish dialogue? Even granting the implausible premise that a Judeo-Christian tradition does not exist, it is still evident that in America our neighbors are Catholics and Protestants, and not Hindus or Moslems. While I for one have no objection to a dialogue with Buddhists, my understanding of my immediate neighbors and their understanding of me seem far more pressing and urgent.

A great Jewish theologian claims that there can be no mutual understanding between Christians and Jews on the level of faith commitment. Jews and Christians, he avers, employ different categories of theological concepts and move within "incommensurable frames of reference and evaluation." This argument would foreclose any communication except with those who have had the same total experience and training that we have had. Is it really impossible for me to grasp the major concepts of Islam? I am not a physician, and yet I have often heard with much profit and interest addresses on medical subjects. Would we deny the possibility of a non-Jew coming from a different historico-cultural community to become a *Ger Tsedek,* a righteous proselyte?

There is no greater spiritual distance than that between Rome and Jerusalem. Yet the Talmud records a number of instances when the Rabbis engaged in "dialogue" with the Romans. Extremely enlightening is the elucidation of a basic Jewish concept by Rabbi Akiba for the benefit of Turnus Rufus, the Roman Governor of Judea, in tractate *Baba Batra:*

> This question was put by Turnus Rufus to Rabbi Akiba: "If your God loves the poor, why does He not support them?" He replied, "So that we may be saved through them from the punishment of Gehinnom." "On the contrary," said the other, "it is this which condemns you to Gehinnom. I will illustrate by a parable. Suppose an earthly king was angry with his servant and put him in prison and ordered that he should be given food and drink, and a man went and gave him food and drink. If the king heard, would he not be angry with him? And you are called 'servants,' as it is written, *for unto Me the children of Israel are servants.*" Rabbi Akiba answered

him: "I will illustrate by another parable. Suppose an earthly king was angry with his son, and put him in prison and ordered that no food or drink should be given to him, and someone went and gave him food and drink. If the king heard of it, would he not send him a present? and we are called 'sons' as it is written, *sons are ye to the Lord your God.*"

Rabbi Akiba brilliantly conveys here to the Roman the Jewish concept of man not as a tool but as a child of God, endowed with infinite worth and dignity.

What Dialogue Is

The danger is that dialogue may degenerate into debate. The real purpose is not to judge or evaluate the faith of one's partner, but rather to clarify and state positions. There is nothing less fruitful or more distressing than a religious debate. Participants should want to understand and be understood, but not to gain a victory or win points.

The demarcation line between debate and dialogue is very thin, a hair's breadth. But then, the sages tell us, the demarcation line between the completely righteous man and the completely evil man is also only a hair's breadth.

Nor is dialogue intended as a "mutual admiration society." Its purpose is not to secure a consensus. Gibbons made the following comment about the attitude of the Romans to religion: "The various modes of worship which prevailed in the Roman world were all considered by the people as equally true; by the philosophers as equally false; and by the magistrate as equally useful." Some of us want so desperately to be agreeable that we forget that our religious commitment lays claim to a truth which is specifically ours. In *Nathan the Wise,* the Friar, impressed with the personality of Nathan, exclaims with admiration: "Nathan, Nathan, you are a Christian; by God you are a Christian. There never was a better Christian." To which Nathan replies, "We are of one mind. For that which makes me in your eyes a Christian, makes you in my eyes a Jew." This may ring pleasantly in our ears, but unfortunately suggests that in order to get along we must be alike. Suppose we differ in important matters? Must we only like the like, and dislike the unlike?

John C. Bennett warns us against a drive for agreement at all costs:

When we think in terms of a common denominator, the danger is that this will become detached from its sources in the particular traditions, that it will become something that exists in and for itself, that it will then become a kind of American sanction and become the fourth religion about which Will Herberg and many critics of our culture speak. There is a danger that interfaith discussions may encourage this secularized fourth religion, that it may become an American religion, that it may lose both the inspiration and the correction which are available in each of our traditions.

The dialogue does not require of us either to underplay our differences or dilute them. We must be honest partners and speak out of deep conviction and commitment. One of the most welcome by-products of the dialogue may very well be the development of a spirit of acceptance of differences as a desirable good.

Toleration of the different is not enough; it suggests a negative value judgment. Dialogue should enable us to see that each faith community must be true to itself at its best, and thereby make its own unique contribution to the spiritual well-being of America. It is not in the sterility and drabness of enforced or agreed-upon uniformity that America will find its best expression, but rather in the richness of the cultural and spiritual differences of its faith communities.

Who Should Participate

Who should participate in dialogue? Participants should obviously be men of good will. But good will alone is not enough. Those who will enter into dialogue must know what they are talking about. One of the basic requirements is therefore for each partner to learn more about himself. It is bad enough when a Jew is fuzzy about his own heritage among his own people; it is disastrous for him to enter into dialogue with others without a solid basis and background of knowledge of Judaism.

If Jews are to take dialogue seriously they must first clarify for themselves the ideas and ideals of Judaism. As long as they lived in isolation there was no need for a sharp and clear-cut definition of Jewish values. They could somehow muddle through without giving definitive answers to many pressing questions. Dialogue demands a greater measure of scholarship and self-knowledge. One of the most important fruits of dialogue might well be an increase in study on the part of Jews of their own spiritual and cultural values.

On the formal, structural level, participants in theological discussions should be scholars and educators competent to speak with authority. It should be made clear, however, that they speak as individuals rather than as representatives of institutions.

In addition, many informal dialogues are taking place among laymen, especially among young people of college age. Since the very spirit of our times seems to generate opportunities for informal dialogue, this call might well become for the Jewish community an occasion to organize an educational program which might prepare adults and young people for more effective participation.

Only those who have a deep commitment to their faith should participate in dialogue. Too often, in the past, interfaith meetings have been what someone described wittily as occasions when Jews who do not believe in Judaism meet Christians who do not believe in Christianity and they find that they have much in common. A philosophical or nostalgic interest in Judaism or Christianity is not enough. Faith should be a way of living rather than a way of talking.

Goals for Dialogue

The distinction has been made by some Jewish leaders between dialogue for social action and dialogue on theological matters. This is a forced, unnatural dichotomy. Judaism does not recognize separate secular and sacred domains: all of life is infused with holiness and every act in the final analysis can be traced to its spiritual roots. In addition, any form of social action must be an outgrowth of our religious view of God, man and society. The discussion about prayer in the public schools may, on the surface, seem to be a civic discussion revolving around the issue of the American political doctrine of the separation of Church and State. Jews are opposed to prayer in the public school because the Jewish concept of prayer as preparation for life, self-judgment and communication with God and with one's better self requires a certain time, place and atmosphere. Rote recital of a neutral formula under the guidance of someone who may not even believe in prayer serves the very opposite goal which prayer is designed to achieve. It is concern for the sacredness and meaningfulness of prayer, and not only or even primarily the principle of the separation of Church and State, that motivates Jewish opposition to prayer in public schools.

Dialogue in the field of social concern would eventually lead us also to dialogue in the field of theological concepts. This should not, however, deter us from discussing matters of public interest upon which we may not agree. At least our positions will become clear and we shall not be misunderstood. If we cannot agree in certain areas such as birth control or public aid to non-public schools, let us at least clarify to each other the basis for our disagreement, and this will help us to disagree agreeably.

While consensus and agreement are not the primary goals of dialogue, many areas of agreement are bound to emerge out of an exchange of views conducted in the spirit of good faith and mutual trust. This will be achieved not through frontal attack upon, and capture of, our partner's positions but rather through a sincere groping for understanding of the points of view involved.

In such areas as the battle for civil rights, the fight against poverty and all forms of prejudice and inequity in our social structure, Jews and Christians can give great strength to each other. Lay people informed and inspired by their respective faith commitments can join together in programs of action. The religious community can thus speak with a united voice and become a powerful force for social good. Planning and working together in dialogue in the field of basic community responsibilities can bring our laymen to a greater understanding and respect of their own faith commitments which provided them in the first place with the dynamism and rationale of their concern.

Dialogue can also bear witness that religion has a stake in society, that it is a relevant and powerful force for social betterment. Dialogue can thus enable us to work together toward "perfecting the world under the kingdom of the Almighty."

❧

Martin Buber on Jews and Christians

What have we and you in common? If we take the question literally, a book and an expectation.

To you the book is a forecourt; to us it is the sanctuary. But in this place we can dwell together, and together listen to the voice that speaks here. That means that we can work together to evoke the buried speech of that voice; together we can redeem the imprisoned living word.

Your expectation is directed toward a second coming, ours to a coming which has not been anticipated by a first. To you the phrasing of world history is determined by one absolute midpoint, the year zero; to us it is an unbroken flow of tones following each other without a pause from their origin to their consummation. But we can wait for the advent of the One together, and there are moments when we may prepare the way for Him together.

The Way of Response: Martin Buber
Selections from His Writings
Edited by Nahum N. Glatzer
(Schocken, 1963)

The Interreligious Dialogue:

Three Jewish Pioneers

Walter Jacob

A quiet revolution has been taking place in American religious life. For a number of years Protestants and Catholics have carried on theological discussions of basic doctrines in a real effort to understand each other.

Jews have made strong efforts to explain themselves to Christians in a voluminous apologetic literature on the tenets, history and ritual of Judaism. But, by and large, Jewish attempts to study Christianity have been limited to historical and scholarly works of men like Joseph Klausner and Samuel Sandmel or to the sociological approach of Will Herberg or to brief sermons. There are as yet few theological studies which treat all of Christianity from a Jewish point of view. Thus far Jewish participation has been hesitant and tentative, growing perhaps out of a certain historic distrust of Christianity, an unwillingness to study Christian writings, and the fear of assimilation.

Current efforts continue those made earlier in the century when rabbis and ministers shared pulpits for the first time and thus expressed their mutual good will. They spoke well of each other's faith and stressed the Judeo-Christian heritage. Laboring together on matters of social justice, they joined hands in battling for the rights of the workingman and improving the status of American politics. The cooperation was genuine and accustomed both clergy and laity to the fact that joint action on practical matters was possible and desirable. In accordance with the American pattern, the beginning took place on the practical level while the theoretical basis was purposely neglected. What, after all, was to be gained from quoting doctrinal statements which divide when the goal was practical reform about which there could be no argument? Biblical statements held in common by all faiths were acclaimed and the rest forgotten.

The next generation continued those efforts but sought to accomplish more. Controversial issues were slowly brought forth and discussed with candor: church and state, religion in the public schools, shared time, birth control have been debated freely by members of the three faiths. Considerable interest has been shown in these practical matters in which some cooperation could be predicated from the outset.

An even higher level of understanding has become possible today—the examination of one another's doctrines and theology. Though the beginnings have been hesitant, true "dialogue" has now became a major theme of American religious life.

American churchmen are not universally enthusiastic about such "dialogue," some barely tolerating it as a temporary movement which need not involve them or their churches. But major liberal forces in every church favor this new path of the "interfaith idea."

Thus far, however, only few modern Jewish thinkers have thoroughly discussed Christianity; most significant among them are Claude Montefiore, Leo Baeck, and Martin Buber. An analysis of their work may help us toward participation in the inter-religious "dialogue."

Claude G. Montefiore

Claude G. Montefiore (1858-1938), a member of a noble British family which has supported Judaism and Jewish causes through many generations by personal scholarship and financial contributions, combined the best of Judaism with the highest values of Western culture. He pursued Jewish studies throughout his life, counting Israel Abrahams, Solomon Schechter, Herbert Loewe and other scholars among his friends. He participated in the effort made at the beginning of the century to discover the rabbinic elements of the New Testament. Along with Robert T. Herford, Hermann Strack and Paul Billerbeck, he helped to demonstrate the interrelationship of early Christian and rabbinic thought. His works show a thorough knowledge of Christianity as well as a fine understanding of Rabbinic Judaism.

Montefiore was a pioneer in his willingness to engage in Christian studies, an area considered dangerous by Jews. Even after a century of emancipation most Jewish attitudes toward Christianity were ambiguous: while the anti-Semitism of many churches kept hatred of Jews alive, at the same time churches sought converts, offering Jews the opportunity to improve their economic and social positions. It was natural for rabbis like Abraham Geiger to look upon Christianity with a jaundiced eye. Yet Montefiore approached Christianity with friendship and understanding because he felt that times had changed on both sides. It was now possible for Christians to look at Judaism in a new way, he felt, because "the number of 'essential doctrines' had gradually diminished."

The nature of Judaism had also changed, particularly liberal Judaism, which saw all religions as constantly growing phenomena. "We have to look upon the New Testament, not dogmatically, but historically," wrote Montefiore. We need not limit ourselves to the verses of the New Testament which offend us: "because one book or chapter of the New Testament conflicts with our highest conceptions of God, it does not follow that another book or another chapter may not consort with them." Montefiore further found rabbinic parallels for the best and most appealing elements of the Gospels.

Even from the writings of Paul, Montefiore extracted elements not necessarily offensive to Jews. "In spite of Paul's amazing forgetfulness of the Jewish doctrine of repentance and atonement, in spite, too, of the remoteness for us of the opposition 'Law versus Christ,' we may still admire the profundity of his genius and adopt many true and noble elements of his religious and ethical teaching. If we can exercise a careful eclecticism in Deuteronomy and Isaiah, we can also exercise it in the Epistle to the Romans and the Corinthians."

Montefiore's discussion of Paul, in a number of essays, partially overcame a major obstacle in better understanding between Christians and Jews. Paul's view of Judaism, particularly the rabbinic Talmud, is disparaging. Montefiore attempted to show that there was no similarity between the Judaism of the Talmud and that attacked by Paul. The religion of which Paul spoke was "poorer, more pessimistic . . . it possessed these inferiorities—just because it was not Rabbinic Judaism, but Diaspora Judaism." Paul's "religion was less intimate and joyous than Rabbinic Judaism, on the one hand, and more theoretic and questioning, upon the other." These views have since been given a sounder foundation by the New Testament scholar Samuel Sandmel.

Montefiore recommended a similar attitude toward Jesus, whose claims to Messianism were of course rejected, as were the doctrines woven around his historic person. But this should not hinder an appreciation of the ethical and moral elements of Jesus' teaching. In general, Montefiore believed that Jews should look at the New Testament and appreciate its best portions. "Liberal Judaism does not teach that all goodness and truth in religion are or can be contained within one book,"

Montefiore maintained. Its equilibrium and fundamental tenets are not upset if the Jews who composed the New Testament, amid much error, said also several things that were new and true. The Jews who wrote the Talmud did the same."

The contribution of Montefiore was a spirit of friendliness and objectivity. A loyal Jew, he was able to view the New Testament rationally and without polemic, and thus approach Christianity with genuine kindness and the will to understand.

Leo Baeck

Another view of Christianity and its basic teachings has been presented by the German scholar and rabbi, Leo Baeck (1872-1956). A life-long student of Christianity, he entered this field through a desire to correct the erroneous view of Judaism given by the Protestant theologian Adolf Harnack in *Das Wesen des Christentums:* his own book *Das Wesen des Judentums* (1905) was not directly concerned with Christianity, but intended to present a thoughtful theological analysis of Judaism to offset Harnack's views.

Baeck frequently dealt with Christianity in essays, later, which were collected in *Aus Drei Jahrtausenden* (1936) and *Wege im Judentum* (1933), the best of which have been translated in *Judaism and Christianity* (1958). Baeck's approach to Christianity was completely different from that of Montefiore. Instead of trying to discover similarities between the two religions, he considered it his duty to clarify their basic differences.

Like Montefiore, he dealt with the problems presented by Paul's attitude toward Judaism. He sought to discover the roots of Paul's anti-legalism in the relationship of Paul and the Talmudic idea of "periods" of history. He pointed out that Paul could only have believed in Jesus as Messiah if he accepted the Talmudic thought that the "period of law" had passed and the period of the Messiah had come. This explains Paul's continuous attack on Rabbinic Judaism. Through his essays, Baeck provided the scholarly background for understanding Christianity. Implied in each was the thought that our generation needed basic distinctions between the major faiths stressed rather than avoided.

A long analysis of Christian theology was undertaken by Baeck in his essay on "Romantic Religion," a powerful polemic piece contrasting the weak elements of "romantic" Christianity with the strength of "classic" Judaism. In a frank manner Baeck deals with the major elements of Christian theology.

Baeck abandoned the apologetic note sounded by his forbears and though such militant writing hardly seems appropriate for the "dialogue," this represents the sincere feeling of a Jew about Christianity. True "dialogue" can never take place if it is limited to uncontroversial statements; it requires an atmosphere of equality. Baeck personally labored toward better relations between Christians and Jews; his essays must be considered as part of that task. Although he had endured the hardships of years spent in a concentration camp, he renewed the attempt to bridge the gap between Jews and Germans after World War II. He expressed the opinions and thoughts of Jews in a polite but firm manner.

Martin Buber

A similar German background produced the great modern Jewish thinker Martin Buber (1878-1965), well known for his re-interpretation of Hasidism and for his "I and Thou" philosophy. Buber's studies of Christianity occupied him for more than 40 years. He dealt with historical and theological problems presented by Christianity, as well as with our current attitude toward that religion. His basic work on this theme, *Two Types of Faith,* presents a new approach to the problem of Paul and his attitude toward Judaism: a distinction between the faith of Jesus and that of Paul. While the former represented the Biblical pattern of faith (*emunah*), the latter followed the Greek idea of faith in a proposition. The faith of Jesus was broad in character and dealt with the fears of the entire people of Israel; Paul was primarily interested in the individual and his salvation through the mysterious Christ. Buber also points out that in Judaism Law represents the relationship between God and man, directing all of man's attention toward the divine. Law remained for Paul an external matter of secondary importance which could not be fulfilled and therefore only created difficulties for man. In the religion of Paul the intimate approach to God, which is the essence of Judaism, was destroyed; this is a distinction between the two faiths which is basic to all the others discussed in the book. Buber agrees with Montefiore and Baeck that the problems presented by Paul remain the main obstacle in all discussions of Christianity.

Buber's fundamental approach is one of deep friendship and respect.

> From my youth onwards I have found in Jesus my great brother . . . I am more than ever certain that a great place belongs to him in Israel's history of faith and that this place cannot be described by any of the usual categories. Under history of faith I understand the history of the human part, as far as known to us, in that which has

taken place between God and man. . . There is something
in Israel's history of faith which is only to be understood
from Israel, just as there is something in the Christian
history of faith which is only to be understood from Christianity. The latter I have touched only with the unbiased
respect of one who hears the Word.

That in this book I have more than once corrected
erroneous representations of the Jewish history of faith
rests upon the fact that these have found their ways into
works of important Christian theologians of our day who
are in other respects authoritative for me. Without sufficient clarification of that which has to be clarified men
will continue to speak to each other at cross-purposes.

Hardly any other Jewish writer has expressed himself with
such kindness about Christianity. Buber remains optimistic
about future relations between the two faiths.

Pre-Messianically our destinies are divided. Now to the
Christian the Jew is the incomprehensibly obdurate man,
who declines to see what has happened; and to the Jew
the Christian is the incomprehensibly daring man, who
affirms in an unredeemed world that its redemption has
been accomplished. But it does not prevent the common
watch for a unity to come to us from God . . . It behooves
both you and us to hold inviolably fast to our own true
faith, that is to our own deepest relationship to truth. It
behooves both of us to show a religious respect for the
true faith of the other. This is not what is called "tolerance," our task is not to tolerate each other's waywardness
but to acknowledge the real relationship in which both
stand to the truth.

Buber has brought us closest to the position necessary to
participation in the "dialogue" with Christianity. He has continued the older efforts to remove misconceptions about Judaism, the Jewish concept of God, and the Hebrew Bible. He has
tried to discover a new approach to the problems which the
New Testament presents to Judaism, and hoped for genuine
discussions between the two religions.

The "dialogue" holds great promise for the future of interfaith relations among Protestants, Catholics and Jews. Through
it our common efforts at understanding may find a theological
basis. The foundation for the participation of Judaism has
been laid by Montefiore, Baeck and Buber.

Questions
Christians Ask

Milton Steinberg

Q. *What are the unique aspects of the Jewish religion?*
A. No less than seven strands weave together to make it up:
1. A doctrine concerning God, the universe, and man;
2. A morality for the individual and society;
3. A regimen of rite, custom, and ceremony;
4. A body of law;
5. A sacred literature;
6. Institutions through which the foregoing find expression;
7. The people, Israel—central strand out of which and about which the others are spun.
    Most of these seemingly distinct threads are in reality different organs of the same creature, animated by a common spirit, reaching into and penetrating one another, no more to be isolated than the parts of a body.

Q. *How do Jews approach the Bible—e.g., the Five Books of Moses, referred to by the Jews as the Torah?*
A. As a physical object the Torah is a parchment sheet, or rather a succession of parchment sheets sewn together breadthwise and rolled about two wooden poles so as to make twin cylinders. These sheets contain the Hebrew original, hand-inscribed and painstakingly edited for absolute accuracy, of the first five books of Scripture.

These questions were formulated by the late Rabbi Morris Adler, based on queries by Christian visitors to Shaarey Zedek in Detroit. The answers are adapted from Rabbi Steinberg's *Basic Judaism* (Harcourt Brace, cloth and paper).

In form the Torah is a narrative, an account of events from the creation of the world to the death of Moses. Between these limits it describes the origins of the nations of the earth and, with especial attention, the beginnings of the people of Israel, the lives of the Patriarchs, the enslavement of the Jews in Egypt, their deliverance and the revelations of God's will which came to them in the wilderness of Sinai.

But the Torah is much more than a narrative.

Among other things it sets forth, if not systematically at least most vividly, a doctrine concerning a one and universal God: the Creator of all things, the Lawgiver, Liberator, and Redeemer of men.

It prescribes rituals, holy days, and festive seasons, together with pertinent forms of worship and observance.

It promulgates a code of law, ecclesiastical, civil, and criminal.

It ordains institutions, religious, domestic, social, philanthropic, and political.

It propounds a conception of the Jewish people as a "kingdom of priests and a holy nation," through whom all the families of the earth are to be blessed.

Q. *What is the Jewish view of revelation? Is there a single view?*

A. Torah, the bond uniting religious Jews, is also the theme of their most fundamental disagreement, the continental divide, as it were, at which traditionalist and modernist begin their divergence.

Traditionalists believe the whole Torah to be God-revealed, therefore unimpeachably true and good throughout.

Modernists hold that truth and goodness are to be found in the Torah, and that to the extent of their presence it is God-inspired.

To traditionalists the entire Torah-Book, every word, every letter, was imparted by God either directly to the whole people of Israel at Mount Sinai or indirectly through Moses. The fact of revelation is decisive. It is a guarantee of absolute validity, intellectual and moral.

To the modernist the first criterion of the truth of a proposition or of the validity of a principle is not its conformity with the tradition but its consonance with reason and experience. Far from judging all things by the standard of Torah, he tests Torah against the standards by which he judges everything else. And only in so far as Torah passes muster does he accept it as authoritative.

This momentous distinction between modernist and traditionalist stems from an even more basic difference: over the susceptibility of Judaism to fundamental change.

The modernist has been persuaded by the biological and social sciences that the law of change is universal —that Judaism is no exception to it; that it is no fixed and constant entity but the end product of a long and still continuing growth.

Even the Torah-Book, according to the modernist, did not come into being all at one time, as the work of Moses. It achieved its familiar shape and dimensions only as the result of an evolutionary process. The typical modernist follows higher criticism in the conclusion that the Torah text as we now have it is a composite of several documents done by diverse authors and sewn into unity by some unknown editor or editors.

Q. *Are there dogmas in Judaism? Do all Jews have the same beliefs?*

A. Judaism does in fact have a very definite religious outlook.

But it is also true that Judaism has been chary about translating its outlook into precise propositions, avoiding dogmas so far as it could; and that for good and sufficient reasons.

Judaism requires formal creed less than do other faiths. For the Jews are not only congregants of a church, they are also members of a historic people and participants in its culture. They are Jews for other reasons than doctrine alone. Unlike Christians in their various sects, Jews can afford considerable latitude on matters of creed. Their group existence does not depend on it so immediately.

Then, too, the beginnings of Judaism were not doctrinal, but historical.

To a unique degree among historic religions, Judaism has cherished and encouraged freedom of thought. Its libertarianism is in part the result of necessity. Jewish theological opinion has always ranged far and wide.

Most important, Judaism has never arrived at a creed because, highly as it rates the life of reason, it rates the good life even higher. For all its heavy intellectualism it sets morality above logic, the pursuit of justice and mercy over the possession of the correct idea.

Q. *How does Judaism approach God?*

A. The primary assertion the Jewish religion makes concerning God is the very cornerstone of Jewish theology: *God is one.*

Judaism says further concerning God:
—That He is the *Creator* of all things through all time.
—That He is *Spirit,* which is to say, that He is at one
  and the same time a Mind that contemplates and a
  Power at work.
—That He is *Lawgiver*.
—That He is the *Guide of History*.
—That He is man's *Helper*.
—That He is the *Liberator* of men and their societies.

Q. *Do Jews really believe they are the "Chosen People"? What
role does the covenant play?*

A. Judaism includes a faith *in* Israel, in the significance of
the role of the Jewish people in history.

The Election is the doctrine that God chose Israel out
of all the nations to be the recipient of His revelation, the
central figure in the drama of human salvation.

Why this people in particular?

In part because of the merits of the first fathers, whose
righteousness was so great as to win this high calling
for their descendants.

In part also because, according to one rabbinic theory,
only this people was willing to accept the disciplines and
hardships incidental to being elected.

The Covenant is the agreement between God and Israel.

As the word implies, the agreement is bilateral. If God
selected Israel, Israel consented to be selected, and in
that fact may be said not only to have been chosen by
God, but to have chosen Him in turn.

Under the terms of their mutual understanding, Israel
as one contracting party undertakes to do God's will without reckoning cost or consequence. God, for His part,
makes Israel His particular treasure, a people near to Him.

No more exalted honor can be conceived than the
Election. But it bestows no special privileges. Quite the
reverse. It entails obligations and hardships.

More, not less, is expected of Israel by virtue of its
unique station. Tribes ignorant of God and His will or
uncommitted to them may be forgiven impieties and sins.
Not so a kingdom of priests and a holy nation which has
given its solemn, pledged word: "All that the Lord hath
spoken will we do and obey."

Q. *How do Jews feel toward non-Jews?*

A. According to the tradition, all men, regardless of race, religion, or nationality are equally God's children, equally

precious in His sight, equally entitled to justice and mercy at the hands of their fellows. Except by virtue of character and conduct, no man is better than any other.

Judaism is totally unaware of race. Though the tradition loves to trace the House of Israel to the Patriarchs, blood descent is no factor in its calculations. Anyone accepting the Jewish faith becomes "a child of Abraham our father" and a "son of Israel" of equal worth with all others.

Q. *What is the Jewish attitude toward conversion?*
A. No one is debarred from conversion because of national or ethnic origins. Judaism has high standards for the admission of proselytes, but they are entirely theological, ethical, ritualistic, and educational.

Anyone may become a Jew; but no one has to do so in order to be saved, whether in this world or the next.

Q. *What is the Jewish attitude toward other faiths?*
A. To the modern Jew, it is good that religions are plural, just as it is advantageous to the world that there are many persons and civilizations.

Each faith is stimulated by the others and is spurred constantly by their criticism to self-purification.

For the Jewish modernist Judaism is wonderfully dowered with merits of the highest order: lucidity and reasonableness in doctrine, exaltation yet practicality in ethic, a passion for social justice, balance between body and soul, a wealth of poetic rituals, dedication of freedom of conscience, reverence for the life of reason, and others in addition.

But any religion may share in some of these qualities, or display still others which Judaism lacks.

Brahmanism has gone much further in exploring the mystic way and in evolving techniques of discipline.

Quakerism has worked out in greater detail the ethics of peaceableness.

Roman Catholicism is more elaborate and dramatic ritually.

The end of the matter is this: the Jewish modernist prefers not to put religions in contrast with one another. He is content that each has its share of verity and worth, that all have the right to be, that out of their diversity, God, man and the truth are better served in the long run.

As for himself, he is at peace in Judaism.

Q. *What is the Jewish attitude toward Jesus?*
A. The query is unanswerable for the reason that there is no

one Jesus but many, according to the number of churches in Christendom. But let us circumvent the impasse by recasting our question. Let us ask: "What do Jews think of the Jesus of the Gospels?"

To Jews, that Jesus appears as a beautiful and noble spirit, aglow with love and pity for men, especially for the unfortunate and lost, deep in piety, of keen insight into human nature, endowed with a brilliant gift of parable and epigram, an ardent Jew moreover, a firm believer in the faith of his people; all in all, a dedicated teacher of the principles, religious and ethical, of Judaism.

But is he not something more than a teacher? Should he not be taken for a moral prophet also, one who promulgated new, higher, hitherto unknown principles of conduct?

Not if the record is examined objectively. The signal fact about Jesus is that except for some relatively unimportant details, he propounded no ethical doctrine in which the Jewish tradition had not anticipated him. Indeed, what he taught was the Jewish tradition as he had received it from Scripture and the sages. For every principle he preached, for many of the epigrams and parables he struck off, Biblical or rabbinic precedent exists. The very phrases of the Sermon on the Mount can be paralleled one by one from the Jewish devotional literature of his time.

Q. *Where does Judaism differ from Christianity?*

A. It was Paul who was mainly responsible for the emergence of Christianity as a new, distinct religion.

With the bulk of the ideas and ideals of Jesus, Judaism is in deep accord.

The Pauline elements in Christianity to which Judaism has objected ever since are:

—The insistence that the flesh is evil and to be suppressed;

—The notion of original sin and damnation from before birth of all human beings;

—The conception of Jesus not as a man but as God made flesh;

—The conviction that men can be saved vicariously, that indeed this is the only fashion in which they can be saved, and that Jesus is God's sacrifice of His only begotten son so that by believing in him they may be saved;

—The abrogation of the authority of Scripture and the tradition, and the nullification of the commandments of the Torah;

—The faith that Jesus, having been resurrected from the dead, bides his time in Heaven until the hour is come for him to return to earth to judge mankind and establish God's Kingdom;

—The final and climactic doctrine that he who earnestly believes these things is automatically saved, but that he who denies them, no matter how virtuous otherwise, is lost to eternal perdition.

Q. *Where do Jews stand on the crucial social issues of our day?*

A. On the evidences of the past and of the modern rabbinate, Judaism stands these days:

—For the fullest freedom, political, economic, and social, for every individual and group, which includes among other things, maximal civil liberties, trade unionism, the equality of all;

—For the social use of wealth, though whether this involves social *ownership* and if so to what extent is disputed among contemporary interpreters of Judaism;

—For a society based on co-operation as its root rule rather than competition;

—For international peace guaranteed by a world government, the notion of the absolute sovereignty of the national state having always been an obscenity in the eyes of the tradition.

Q. *To what extent is the rabbi a source of authority?*

A. Rabbis are teachers of the tradition. They are generally called on to discharge additional functions as pastors, preachers, administrators, and communal leaders. But first and foremost they are teachers. This is the essence of their being.

To say of rabbis that they are teachers is to deny that they are priests. Unlike some other religions, Judaism does not assert of its clergy that they possess spiritual powers, conferred either by ordination or vocation, which are inaccessible to the laity. In its eyes no difference exists, except in training, between the man at the pulpit and those in the pews. Nor is there any rite at all which only the former can properly perform. Any layman who has the knowledge and the spiritual fitness may conduct worship and, if he has something to say and can get a congregation to listen to him, may preach.

Rabbis, further, are not "called," as some evangelical denominations understand the word. It is not required of them that they undergo a mystical experience of illumination or of selection by Providence for the ministry.

They are, of course, expected to enter the rabbinate in the spirit of self-consecration; to be good people, genuine as to belief and principle, ardently devoted to the tradition and to the service of God, Israel, and mankind. But all these qualities Judaism hopes to find in every Jew; none of them belongs peculiarly to the rabbinate. In the end then the rabbi differs from his Jewish fellows only in being more learned than they, more expert in the tradition they all share. He is a rabbi by virtue of education; his ordination is a graduation, his title an academic degree.

Q. *Do Jews believe in life after death?*
A. Death cannot be and is not the end of life.

Man transcends death in many altogether naturalistic fashions. He may be immortal biologically, through his children; in thought, through the survival of his memory; in influence, by virtue of the continuance of his personality as a force among those who come after him; and ideally, through his identification with the timeless things of the spirit.

When Judaism speaks of immortality it has in mind all these. But its primary meaning is that man contains something independent of the flesh and surviving it; his consciousness and moral capacities, his essential personality: a soul.

As to the form of the hereafter, of the Paradise or Heaven or Eden where righteousness is said to be rewarded, of the Hell or Sheol or Gehinnom where wickedness is punished—on this, as on so many other articles of belief, individual Jews have at all times put private interpretations. Indeed, it is questionable whether any other tenet of Judaism has been more divergently construed.

Q. *What is the Jewish belief about the Messiah?*
A. The Messiah is the human being appointed by God and armed by Him with the power and authority to purge the world of its evils and to establish the good upon foundations so firm as never to be moved. He is that descendant of David of whom the prophet spoke when he said:

There shall come forth a shoot out of the stock of Jesse,
And a twig shall grow forth out of his roots.
And the spirit of the Lord shall rest upon him,
The spirit of wisdom and understanding,
The spirit of counsel and might,
The spirit of knowledge and of the fear of the Lord.

The tradition holds that the world's redemption is to be effected by a single man in one climactic episode.

About this basic faith the Jewish spirit has woven variants innumerable. Some Jews have imagined the Messiah as a mystical superman, others on the other hand as little more than an exceptionally skilled, virtuous, and successful statesman.

Messiah is always envisaged as a man, even by those who would invest him with extraordinary powers. Never is he supposed to be a God. Again, it is assumed of him that only he can bring lasting deliverance to Israel and the nations.

What then remains for men to do for human redemption? Whatever comes to hand; whatever they can. But with their efforts they must hope, pray, and wait for the Messiah. Only with his aid can victory be won in completeness, the regeneration of men and the transmuting of society being tasks too great for ordinary mortals.

Modernists, to speak paradoxically, believe in a Messianic Age but not in a personal Messiah, not even when he is conceived in the most naturalistic terms. Nor do they doubt the power of mankind to bring the Kingdom into being.

Wherefore, modernists hold, the Messiah is not one man. Rather are all good men messiahs since by laboring together they cause the Kingdom to come. Nor will it arrive all at once. It will be achieved slowly, cumulatively, "precept by precept, line by line, here a little, there a little." Indeed, there is a sense in which it will never be altogether achieved.

And God, where is He in this process as the modernist envisages it?

He is, as always, at work in men, in their hopes and aspirations, in the skill and fortitude with which they pursue them.

When then the Kingdom has come at last, when the final evil has been broken and the remotest good achieved, the glory of that moment will belong to all the men past and present who have dreamed of it and striven toward it.

But the deeper glory will belong to Him who through the ages has spurred mankind, often against its will, to the greater good and beyond that to the greatest.

In that hour men, departed and living alike, will have abundant reason to chant together the litany of the Psalmist:

"Not unto us, O Lord, not unto us, but unto Thy name give glory."

Questions Jews Ask

Solomon S. Bernards

Q. *How many Americans are affiliated with Christian churches today? How is affiliation reckoned? What about other un-affiliated, non-Jewish Americans: are they Christians?*

A. The research staff of the National Council of Churches estimates that of a total American population of 190 million, 118 million are members of various Christian denominations and churches.

Affiliation is counted in any number of ways. Roman Catholics count all persons, including infants who have been baptized under Catholic auspices. Some Protestant communions follow the Catholic practice, but most count only persons 13 years and over, who are on the active roster. The Eastern Orthodox count all people within their ethnic group, while Negro churches keep very informal records.

We tend to characterize all non-Jewish Americans as Christians. This is inaccurate, not only because there are Buddhists, Islam followers and others, but also because there are atheists and agnostics who do not consider themselves Christians, though they may come from Christian homes or forbears. There are also Unitarian-Universalists, Ethical Culture-ists, Humanists and other groups. Public opinion polls indicate that 95-98 percent of the American people say they believe in God.

Based on queries most frequently received, answers have been culled by Rabbi Bernards from standard Christian sources.

Q. *What are the main branches of American Christianity, and what are their numbers?*

A. There are three principal groupings: Protestants, Roman Catholics and Eastern Orthodox. The Protestants number approximately 69 million, divided into about 250 different denominations. The Roman Catholic Church, with some 46 million adherents, is the largest, strongest single church body. The Eastern Orthodox churches count about 3.2 million in some 20 groups.

Within the Protestant denominations, there are the following principal "mainstream churches": Southern Baptists (10.8 million), Methodists (10.4 million), Lutherans (9.0 million), Negro Baptists (9.0 million), Episcopalians (3.4 million), Presbyterians (Northern) (3.4 million), Negro Methodist denominations (2.3 million), United Church of Christ (2.1 million), Christian Churches (Disciples) (2.0 million), Greek Archdiocese of North and South America (1.7 million), Northern Baptists (1.5 million), Southern Presbyterians (900,000).

In addition, there are 2.4 million Evangelicals (loosely federated groups of fundamentalists, intensively mission-minded bodies), Seventh Day Adventists, Pentacostals, Mormons (1.8 million), Quakers (Society of Friends), Christian Scientists, Jehovah Witnesses, Mennonites and Reformed Churches.

Q. *What do Christians believe about Jesus of Nazareth?*

A. Roman Catholics, Eastern Orthodox and most Protestants are Trinitarians. This distinctive doctrine of Christian faith asserts that the Godhead consists of three persons: the Father, the Son and the Holy Ghost. Trinitarians believe that God took upon Himself the form of a human being in Jesus. This is called the Doctrine of the Incarnation.

The Glock-Stark survey, *Christian Beliefs and Anti-Semitism*, part of the five-year study of anti-Semitism conducted at the University of California under a grant from the ADL, verified the overwhelming commitment of American Christians to a belief in Jesus as the Divine Son of God, even though as many as 28 percent in one denomination had doubts about it. Roman Catholics scored a total of 94 percent, Southern Baptists and Missouri Lutherans, 99 and 98 percent respectively, down to a total of 68 percent for Congregationalists.

In the past few years, a group of Protestant theologians have caused a stir with the "death of God" controversy, in which it is insisted that God is dead but that Jesus persists as the perfect man.

The Unitarian position on Jesus is explained by Rev. Karl Chworowky. "If to be a Christian is to profess and sincerely seek to practice the religion of Jesus, so simply and beautifully given in the Sermon on the Mount, then Unitarians are Christians. But because Unitarians do not acknowledge Jesus as their "Lord and Savior," they are often thought of as being non-Christian and, in fact, are not eligible for membership in the National Council of Churches."

Closely related to the belief in the divinity of Jesus is the concept of finality and exclusivity of the revelation of Jesus, which insists that the last word as to the salvation of all humanity has been said in the Christian Gospels, that no other way to the redemption of humankind is possible, and that the Second Coming of Jesus awaits the embracing of Christianity by the whole human family, including (as one theologian recently suggested) people who may be discovered on other planets.

Q. *What does Christianity teach about the Bible?*
A. To Christians, the term "Bible" includes both the Hebrew Scriptures (what they call the "Old Testament") and the New Testament. The Hebrew Scriptures, in the traditional Christian view, are a foreshadowing, a pre-figuration, a prediction of the coming of Jesus as the Messiah. Christians add many works of the Apocrypha and the Pseudepigrapha, not included in the Hebrew Bible. Protestants differ from Roman Catholics on the books they include both in the Hebrew and Christian segments of the Bible.

The beginning of the Reformation under Martin Luther was associated with the "open Bible," with the replacement of the authority of the Pope with that of the Bible. The Bible is regarded as the primary source of what is true and right, as the major guide to Christian faith and life. Thus, every forward thrust of Protestantism to new lands was accomplished by zealous efforts to translate the Bible into new languages and dialects. Since the missionary efforts of the 19th century, the Bible—mainly the Synoptic Gospels, and particularly the Johanine Gospel according to John—since the latter is a favorite missionary tract— has been translated into over 1200 languages, many of them for which an alphabet and grammar had to be developed by missionary scholars out of the raw material of everyday speech. The Hebrew Scriptures have been translated into over 300 languages.

In spite of much progress in Christian scholarly circles in the study of the Hebrew Bible and a consequent appreciation of the need to deal with it in terms of its own integrity, the literalism and "biblicism" of churchgoers and preachers run very deep. Thus, the Christological interpretation of many passages of the Hebrew Bible, which allegorize the entire Hebrew text into a prediction and foreshadowing of the coming of Jesus, is still widely followed. "The reason for this lag," Frederick C. Grant has observed, "is that most clergymen and teachers consider it hopeless to stem a tide that has been running high for sixteen centuries; they are unwilling to question publicly the traditional biblicism of the churches, including the traditional interpretation of both Old Testament and New."

Q. *What are Christianity's views about Jews and Judaism?*
A. The late Jules Isaac, French-Jewish historian, in his epoch-making essay "Has Anti-Semitism Roots in Christianity?" and in his book *The Teaching of Contempt,* pointed to three main teachings of the Gospels and the Church which he regarded as the sources of Christian anti-Semitism:

a) that Judaism was in a state of degeneration at the time of Jesus; that it was mere legalism without a soul, dessicated, ossified, reduced to mere formalism and ritual. (A study of the Second Commonwealth period shows, to the contrary, that the dynamism and creativity of Judaism were never greater.)

b) that the Jewish people are collectively guilty of the crime of deicide. (This destructive and evil charge has been deplored in the Vatican Declaration on the Non-Christian Religions and condemned in a number of statements by the World Council of Churches, the National Council of Churches, and denominational bodies.)

c) that the dispersion and suffering of the Jewish people are proof positive that God is punishing them for having refused to accept Jesus. (The Diaspora pre-dated Christianity by at least 500 years and is not historically linked to it.)

The Glock-Stark survey, referred to earlier, found an alarmingly high percentage of contemporary church members agreeing that (1) Jews can never be forgiven for what they did to Jesus, unless they accept Christianity, and (2) Jews have suffered through the centuries because God is punishing them for their having rejected Jesus. These invidious notions of Jews, where linked to a syndrome of orthodox and particularistic, exclusivistic views of Christianity, were found almost inevitably to lead to

venomous feelings of anti-Semitism against contemporary
Jews.

Christian writings insisted that the Church had superseded Judaism and the Jewish people in all the preroga-
tives which the Hebrew Scriptures had assigned to the
Jewish people. Jewish history and Jewish living as dynamic
entities were deemed as having disappeared after the triumph of Christianity. Judaism became a "fossil," a relic
—if not dead, not much alive either.

Early in his Reformation efforts, Martin Luther up-
braided the Church for its outrageous conduct toward
Jews while at the same time expecting the Jews to accept
conversion. He counselled gentleness and friendship.
Twenty years later Luther viewed the meager results in
terms of converts which his policy had produced, and he
turned on Jews with an unbelievable fury, far surpassing
his predecessors in his envenomed denunciations of Jews
and Judaism.

Through the centuries, there were Church leaders who
spoke of Judaism and the Jewish community in terms of
appreciation and sympathy. But there remained the persistent, nagging concern for the Jewish soul—the unflag-
ging hope that Jews would one day embrace Christianity.
This missionary zeal injected the poison of suspicion and
distrust in Christian-Jewish relations from earliest times.

Many of the images and conceptions which blocked
genuine interchange between Christians and Jews are
now being re-examined. The pre-conditions of mutual respect and trust are being met so that Jew and Christian
can view each other's commitments, beliefs and hopes,
as they are.

Q. *What do Judaism and Christianity hold in common?*
A. Many things, but principally a vision of the Fatherhood of
God and the brotherhood of man. From the prophetic
utterances of the Hebrew Scriptures came the framework
for the building of the good society: an abiding concern
with justice, love, compassion and the doing of good deeds.
The tradition which formed the background of Jesus and
his disciples, and those who followed them, was based
on a God who cares, whose mercies are over all His
creatures, who made man but little lower than the angels,
and who charged him to be sensitive to the pain of all
living things. Christianity flowed out of a Jewish tradition
which exalted study as a way of life, which urged an embracing of the world and endowed it with a sense of holiness, a recognition of the possibilities of human growth.

The Parting of the Ways

Ellis Rivkin

The question of who crucified Jesus is basically an historical problem. After all, Jesus did live at a point in time. The Jews had been in existence long before Christianity arose, developed and separated itself from the Judaism out of which it had evolved.

The historian's task is to reconstruct the world in which Jesus lived and recognize its dynamic and revolutionary character. This is difficult because the accounts are garbled: the Gospels of Mark, Matthew and Luke do not agree, for the most part, and where they are in agreement, John, the Fourth Gospel, presents a radically different version. No witnesses wrote down what occurred and for a considerable period after Jesus' death the story of his life, message and crucifixion was handed down by word of mouth. The Gospels naturally reflect this general uncertainty.

Because of the geographical location of Palestine, at the juncture point between Egypt and Syria, Persia and Asia Minor, and all the connecting routes to Greece and Rome, the Jews were always a prey for imperialist powers. While the theocracy of the Second Temple was still flourishing, Alexander the Great and his successors brought Hellenistic civilization and a dynamic new kind of Greek city, which affected and changed the countryside, disrupting the even tenor of the agricultural life which had been the mainstay of the theocratic system.

Whereas before the emergence of cities the vast majority of Jews had been peasants, now shopkeepers, artisans, craftsmen, businessmen and merchants emerged. A complex economic and social structure replaced a simple agricultural structure.

Struggling with the problems of life in a new world, the new elements in society could not be content with the fixed and permanent law of the Pentateuch, which was geared primarily to tillers of the soil, and which foreclosed change. The outcome was nothing less than a new orientation toward God, man, religion and destiny—a reorientation which in its way was as significant as the Bible itself—for it emphasized the worth and significance of each single individual human being in the eyes of God. It declared the revolutionary concepts of the twofold Law (Oral and Written), of personal salvation in the world to come, and of the resurrection from the dead.

The Pharisees

The Pharisees, a revolutionary scholar class, daringly formulated these novel and crucial doctrines.

In actuality, the Pharisees got their name* "separatists" because they opposed the theocracy. They were denounced by the theocratic priests, the Sadducees, as having separated themselves from official Judaism. The term Pharisees became the permanent designation, even though they referred to themselves as *soferim* (scribes), *hahamim* (sages) or *zekenim* (elders).

Pharisaism was a movement which sought individual salvation not through the Temple but through a personal religious life, concentrated in the synagogue. In opposition to the theocracy, this movement modified the laws of the Pentateuch and made them operable for people living in a new type of society. For example, although previously it was not permissible to walk outdoors on the Sabbath, the Pharisees or sages permitted people to walk anywhere in the city on that day. When the law was unyielding and unbending, the Pharisees made it pliable and subject to change. They modified the laws of ritual purity for non-priests, first by requiring only a ritual bath and subsequently by legislating that the mere washing of the hands was sufficient.

They recognized, however, that if the law was to change, it had to change through regularized channels. Here is where they came into conflict with Jesus. As the Gospel of Mark (1:22) succinctly states: "And they were astonished at his teaching, for he taught them as one who had authority, *and not as the scribes*" (italics mine). The Pharisees opposed Jesus because they did not believe that any individual should

* *Perushim*, i.e., heretics

change the law merely on the basis of his own personal authority. Jesus' basic difference with the Pharisees was thus over the acceptance of his role. Since the Pharisees refused to recognize Jesus as the Messiah, he looked upon them as having rejected him and his message. Normally, he lived a Pharisaic life, and urged his fellow disciples to do likewise. But when the Pharisaic laws were broken, he refused to consider such violations as important as the rejection by the Pharisees of his message.

The Roman conquest of Palestine brought much suffering. Large numbers of independent Jewish farmers, unable to meet the heavy taxes, lost their land. The notorious policy of "divide and conquer" was put into effect. The Roman procurator was responsible for law and order in Palestine, and he in turn appointed the High Priest, who was responsible for the good behavior of the populace and whose position was dependent on his unswerving loyalty to Rome. At the time of Jesus the High Priest was Caiphas, appointed by Pontius Pilate, who must have been an extraordinarily crafty, cruel and ambitious person, especially sensitive to the slightest stirring against Roman rule; indeed, Josephus, a friend and admirer of Rome, affirms that Pontius Pilate was one of the most vicious of the procurators, repeatedly provoking revolts so that they might be cruelly put down.

Jesus in Rome

Long before the war against Rome (65-70), in response to the troubled time, two different solutions were offered Jews by groups that had broken off from Pharisaism. One, referred to by Josephus as the Fourth Philosophy, called for revolutionary violence against Rome and against those Jews who collaborated with Rome. Its goal was the equality of all men under God.

The second group consisted of apocalyptic visionaries, who forswore violence but preached that the kingdom of God was at hand. Its coming would bring to an end domination, suffering and inequality. Jesus was one of those who preached the imminent coming of the kingdom of God and who called upon his listeners to live the kind of life that would hasten it. Such preachment, though eschewing violence, was revolutionary in character, for it most definitely implied the sweeping away by God of Roman rule.

The High Priest was always on watch for any signs of rebellion. When Jesus came to Jerusalem on the eve of Passover, he was greeted in the streets as the king of the Jews, the son of David. It was festival time and tens of thousands of people were milling around. Pontius Pilate had come from his headquarters with troops, in case of trouble.

And Jesus was causing trouble in that he claimed to be the Messiah. People were referring to him as the descendant of David, which to High Priest Caiphas and the procurator suggested a dynasty, the replacement of Roman rule. What could the kingdom of God mean except the end of the Roman kingdom? Jesus was arrested, not because he was preaching violence but because he was identified with the Davidic dynasty, the Messiah, the kingdom of God, and, as such, threatened the whole Roman system.

Jesus was brought to the High Priest, and was tried before a *sanhedrin* or council made up of Jewish collaborators with Rome. Their decision was rendered not in terms of a law court, a *bet din*, but in terms of whether Jesus was politically dangerous or not.

According to various statements in the Gospel, Pontius Pilate would have saved Jesus. But a closer reading of the account discloses that the procurator repeatedly asked Jesus: "Are you the king of the Jews? Shall I save the king of the Jews?" The word "king" was used provocatively, as a trap. To have asked for Jesus' release would have been equivalent to rebellion.

The Crucifixion

The emblem on the cross which read "King of the Jews" is stark and conclusive evidence that Jesus was crucified because he was viewed as a threat to Roman sovereignty. He was believed to have had Messianic pretensions and therefore deserved, from the Roman point of view, the death of all rebels—crucifixion. The High Priest was the representative not of the Jewish people but of Pontius Pilate, the instrument of Roman domination. If he agreed to Jesus' death, it was to indicate that the Jews were loyal to him and to Caesar. They owed no allegiance to any other king.

Thus the drama of the interplay between oppressors and oppressed becomes clear. The whole Roman system was geared to preventing anyone from emerging who might disrupt its rule. The Roman authorities appointed people like High Priest Caiphas to make sure that their regime would remain. They sought the collaboration of the wealthy.

In crucifying Jesus, the Romans were using a mode of punishment commonly visited on those who in any way indicated any other loyalty or recognized the sovereignty of any other kingdom than that of Caesar. Crucifixion, a daily occurrence in Palestine, was a warning to the discontented.

The question of "Who crucified Jesus?" should therefore be replaced by the question "What crucified Jesus?" What crucified Jesus was the destruction of human rights, Roman imperialism, selfish collaboration. What crucified Jesus was a type of regime which, throughout history, is forever crucifying those who would bring human freedom, insight, or a new way of looking at man's relationship to man. Domination, tyranny, dictatorship, power and disregard for the life of others were what crucified Jesus. If there were among them Jews who abetted such a regime, then they too shared the responsibility.

The mass of Jews, however, who were so bitterly suffering under Roman domination that they were to revolt in but a few years against its tyranny, can hardly be said to have crucified Jesus. In the crucifixion, their own plight of helplessness, humiliation and subjection was clearly written on the cross itself. By nailing to the cross one who claimed to be the Messiah to free human beings, Rome and its collaborators indicated their attitude toward human freedom.

Transformation of Jesus

The next question is how a helpless crucified victim of Roman power became the son of God whose death brought eternal life. How did Jesus, who came as a Messiah for the Jews, become Christ? How did an apocalyptic visionary with a message for the poor, the humble, the downtrodden and rejected of his people become the risen Lord? How did a simple teacher from Galilee become the heir of the Roman Empire and redemptive God for much of mankind?

The historical Jesus belongs to Jews and Judaism even though most Jews rejected his claims, and even though his Judaism was a deviant form of Pharisaism. He came for Jews, he ministered to Jews, he sought to usher in the kingdom of God for Jews, his message was expressed in the language of Judaism, his immediate disciples were Jews. The historical Jesus survives in the Gospels as a human being. His immediate disciples had known him as a Jewish teacher who had come to his fellow Jews with the message of the imminent coming of the kingdom of God; and since they themselves were Jews, they were unable to reconcile a belief in the resurrected Jesus with their intimate knowledge of the Jesus who had healed the sick, driven out the demons, quarreled with the Pharisees, and who had been arrested and crucified.

Paul was the true founder of Christianity. It was he who concentrated on the crucifixion of Jesus and its redemptive meaning, while he ignored the actual life and teachings of Jesus. What Jesus had said was of little consequence; but what had happened to him, for him and by him was the turning point in human history. God the Father had given His son to mankind so that through his death sin itself might be crucified and the believing who had taken on Christ would be resurrected to life eternal. Faith in the redemptive power of Christ was absolutely necessary for salvation; all who believed in the Christ were the true members of Israel.

How did Paul come to such radical conclusions? Why did he reject so totally the Judaism of his earlier years? Paul had been a Pharisee (Philippians 3:4-6; cf. Galatians 1:13-14), he had been a rabid persecutor of the early Christians (Galatians 1:13, Philippians 3:6). Suddenly he was totally transformed. The rest of his life was dedicated to fervent and agitated spread of the gospel of the Christ crucified and the Christ resurrected, and this gospel he preached primarily to the Gentiles.

Ascendancy of Paul

Paul's transformation from persecutor to persecuted, from a zealous devotee of the Law to its annihilator, from a Hebrew of the Hebrews to the apostle to the Gentiles is closely bound up with the character of Pharisaism. The Pharisaic teachers had developed Judaism into a *mitzvah* system of salvation, one that insists that personal salvation in the world to come and resurrection from the dead are dependent on performing the authoritative religious acts.

The *mitzvah* system places responsibility on the individual; it is dependent on internalized authority. The young child incorporates into himself the teaching of his parents as to which *mitzvot* please God and which *averot* (sins) displease Him. Failure to keep the *mitzvot* creates feelings of guilt; their fulfillment gives comfort and reassurance.

But what of an individual whose early life experiences are such that he has difficulty internalizing the religious demands taught by his parents? What if in such a person the wish to overthrow and to defy first parental authority and then God's authority is so powerful that the demands of the *mitzvot* become a relentless source of guilt and pain? Such an individual can fight his rebellious impulses by being over-zealous in the performance of the *mitzvot* and by becoming an arch-persecutor of those who deviate in any way from the *mitzvah* system. Under certain conditions, a complete reversal may occur: the persecutor may then seek persecution; the zealot for *mitzvot* can become the arch enemy of the *mitzvah* system; the champion of the chosen people can turn into an apostle to the Gentiles.

Something of this sort must have happened to Paul. He felt that the Law itself had stirred up within him the wish to sin and violate it. He says that if the Law had not commanded "thou shalt not covet," he would not have felt covetousness. Behind the Law lurked sin. The Law did not destroy the sinful impulses; it evoked them. Only when he had experienced Christ crucified and had freed himself from the Law— only then were the demands of the flesh crucified. Christ had redeemed him from the internal struggle with the demands of the *mitzvah* system and had given him the feeling that he was indeed a new creation. So thorough had been his transformation that he dedicated all his energies to the spread of his gospel (cf. Romans 7; Galatians 2:15-21).

And Paul's gospel touched many an agonized soul in the Mediterranean world. Not that the Gentiles to whom he preached had undergone Paul's experience with the *mitzvah* system of salvation. Indeed, Paul had the least influence over those who lived that system. The Gentiles who were drawn to Paul's teaching benefitted by the emancipation from the Law only in the sense that it was no longer a hindrance to becoming a believer in Christ. The doctrine of Paul that had deep meaning for them was the emphasis on the redemption from sin made possible by God's grace through His son who was crucified so that eternal life would be assured for all those who believed.

Rise of Christianity

Paul's gospel promised triumph over death through identification with the crucified and resurrected Christ. Pauline Christianity uniquely incorporated certain features characteristic of Judaism. The one cosmic yet fatherly God who had revealed His will in Scriptures is preserved by Paul. While the Law of Scriptures is abolished, its promises are used to justify faith in the Christ. So too, the internalized character of Pharisaic Judaism is preserved even though the *mitzvot* are no longer internalized. When one truly accepted Christ, one's whole life was transformed by the Holy Spirit. Salvation was dependent on continually being in Christ. No true Christian was a Christian on a part-time basis. In this sense, Christianity maintained Pharisaism's emphasis on the total character of God's demands.

Similarly, Pauline Christianity preserved the tightly knit social character of Judaism. Every Jew who accepted the *mitzvah* system felt a closeness and responsibility for every other Jew who accepted the binding character of the *mitzvot*, the works commanded by the divinely revealed Written and Oral Law. So too every true Christian considered every other Christian as his brother in Christ and felt a responsibility for his welfare. Like the Jew under the *mitzvah* system, the Christian in Christ visited the sick, clothed the naked, ransomed the captive, buried the dead, aided the poor. Just as the synagogue of Israel expressed the unity of those who sought salvation through *mitzvot*, so the Church of God bound together those who sought salvation through faith in the Christ.

But the Pauline doctrine of the Christ also had close affinities to the mystery cults. Although Christianity was not a mystery cult, some of its doctrines and practices had the appeal of the latter. Jesus could certainly be viewed as a savior God who had lived, died and been resurrected. Like the savior gods of the mystery cult, he could bestow eternal life on those who, through baptism, died with him and who thereby gained immortality through his resurrection. The communal meal of the true Christian believers likewise resembled cultic practices. In eating the bread, Christians ate the body of Christ; in drinking the wine, they drank his blood. In this way Christ entered their bodies and transformed them.

Too much was at stake for the individual to trust his immortality to an untried savior God. Paul pointed to the ancient God of Israel and to his revealed Scriptures as proof that Jesus was the very son of this renowned God and therefore no upstart or usurper. The Christ was the fulfillment of the promise made by God to Abraham, and he was therefore prior even to the giving of the Law (cf. Galatians 3). Thus Jesus was the very embodiment of the eternal God and Father of the Scriptures and of the traditions of the Pharisees.

Links and affinities unquestionably exist which bind Pauline Christianity to both Judaism and the mystery cults. But it was the principle of the redemptive Christ that was ultimately responsible for Christianity's great success. The appeal of the mystery cults with its savior gods and the appeal of Judaism with its one God and Father, its revealed Scriptures, its ethical, moral and social concern, its emphasis on religion as permeating all of life, and its promise of salvation in the future life—these were experienced through the Christ who had died to free man from sin. The actual identification of the true believer with a man-God who had so recently lived and suffered as a human being and yet was the son of the Father God of ancient Judaism was the crucial feature.

Here were the promises of Judaism without the *mitzvah* system; here was the mystery cultic experience without its polytheism, amorality, social disinterestedness; here too was the overcoming of sin, death and suffering through a human God who had personally experienced agony and death for *each* individual. When Rome itself began to collapse in the third century, the message of Christianity seemed the only answer,

Survival of Judaism

Only one other religion was adequate to the problems of a collapsing world, and that was the *mitzvah* system of Judaism. Unlike the pagan mystery cults, Judaism did not succumb to Christianity.

Judaism did not have a savior God, that is, a God that lived, died and was resurrected. The mystery cults did, and yet they were unable to withstand Christianity.

The answer must therefore be sought elsewhere, in the monotheism of Judaism and its *mitzvah* system of salvation. Through Christianity monotheism triumphed over paganism; but Judaism had been the source of Christian monotheism. Judaism was therefore not only adequate to a world organized around monotheistic concepts; it had itself provided the organizing principle.

In itself the montheistic principle is not a sufficient explanation; for the Sadducean rendition of Judaism was likewise monotheistic, yet it did not survive. Monotheism had to be linked to the daily experience of the individual, and the one God also had to be the loving Father who granted salvation to those who followed His will. This will was incorporated in the *mitzvah* system which was the path of individual salvation. Though this integration of monotheism and individual salvation was not capable of winning the souls of the pagan world, it did organize the complex experiences of life in the Greco-Roman world adequately. Its religious system not only withstood the disintegrating forces of the Roman world, but also the integrating powers of triumphant Christianity.

Thus from an historical point of view both Judaism and Christianity were necessarily interlinked in the processes that ultimately dissolved the polytheistic interpretations of human experience. Judaism generated the idea of monotheism welded to individual salvation. Christianity secured the triumph of this idea in the pagan world through its doctrine of the one God and Father who through the Christ crucified and resurrected promised eternal life to every individual soul that believed. Both Judaism and Christianity proved adequate to the demands of the historical process.

Two Roads:
A Christian Reverie

Poul Borchsenius

In my native Denmark, a few miles north of Randers, is an old village called Spenstrup. Its church, also old, was built 800 years ago during the great epoch of the Valdemars. Not many years after its completion, an unknown artist painted a fresco in the triumphal arch which opens up the choir to the congregation. Like most religious pictures of the Catholic period it was painted over when the winds of Reformation blew through the Danish church. About a hundred years ago, however, the picture reappeared beneath the plaster, and it has since been uncovered and restored.

Once seen, the painting is never forgotten. As often as I have stood before it, it moves me anew by its beauty, refined and primitive at the same time. The artist must have had great skill. He used the natural colors of carbon black, ochre, vermilion, verdigris, and the costly blue extracted from lapis lazuli. Although some of its colors have faded, the painting has resisted the ravages of time, and we see it today as the congregation saw it centuries ago.

Uppermost in the picture is the Agnus Dei, the lamb of God, symbol of Christ. Beneath the lamb stand two women, young and beautiful. The woman to the left, representing the Synagogue, has her hair hanging loose over her green robe, while the one to the right wears the robe of a queen under a scarlet coat and represents the Church. The former is blindfolded, since we learn from Paul that she does not see that Jesus is the Savior. She holds a lance in her hand, which she charges into the throat of the lamb, wounding it to death. Blood spurts from the wound, which the woman representing the Church collects in a chalice. Thus, symbolically, as the crown falls from the head of the Synagogue, the Church victoriously steps on the head of the snake fulfilling the prophecy that the seed of woman shall crush its head.

This depiction of the blindfolded Synagogue which loses its crown and the victorious Church, which, with queenly beauty, collects the sacrificial blood, is by no means unique. This is how Church and Synagogue were pictured in the Middle Ages, in famous old churches throughout the Christian countries of Europe. The Cathedral of Strasbourg, for example, has a celebrated painting of the same two women.

So established and widespread was the ecclesiastical judgment concerning the infidelity and punishment of the Synagogue that even a remote village church like that of Randers bears its imprint. Sunday after Sunday for centuries it impressed upon succeeding congregations the image that the Jews murdered Christ and that in the history of salvation the position of Israel has been inherited by the Church.

An echo of doom comes to us from the picture, the alarm —even fear—felt by the old Church at the thought of the Jews and the eternal problem to which their mere existence gave rise. It keeps reverberating in our thoughts long after we leave the church. We are face to face with a riddle.

Two thousand years ago the Church broke away from the Synagogue. The way to God was split into two roads, which since then have run far apart. When Israel denied the New Gospel, God's peoples became disunited, and a gaping abyss of mutual distrust and prejudice has continued to separate the Synagogue from the Church.

The thought of a disbelieving Israel has always haunted the Church. Its first generation was filled with consternation when the New Gospel was denied by the masses of the Jewish people. And when the Church became a world power and the barbarians of Europe bowed to the white Christ, one people tenaciously stuck to its inherited faith: the Jews continued to be Jews. The Church felt insecure whenever the thought of those obdurate deniers crossed its mind. Although they were few in number and their synagogues low and grey, the fact that they denied the central dogma of Christianity and still met life and death with peace of mind invited doubt. Warnings against them had to be issued. The Church formulated its doctrine against Jews with haste and fury. The old fresco in the church reflects what the artist heard monks and ministers preaching. This is what they said:

Once upon a time Israel was the Chosen People, but that was long ago. The crown dropped from its head when the Jews refused to believe in Jesus and had him murdered in their disbelief. When they committed that crime, God took away from Israel its right to primogeniture and handed it to the Church. From that moment Judaism began to shrivel, and now it is a dead religion. The Church is the New Israel. It has taken over everything of value from the old faith. The creative power and divine attributes of Israel belong to the Christian Church today.

The Jews themselves were rejected. God punished them, made them homeless, and scattered them all over the earth. Actually they ought to have been exterminated. If, nevertheless, they continue to exist, it must be because in God's judgment they serve as a lesson to other peoples. Stigmatized as the descendants of Cain, branded as the murderers of God, they are condemned to struggle through a miserable and fearful life. That is the moral of the legend about the eternal Jew who mocked Jesus on the road to Golgatha, and who wanders from country to country with no place to rest.

The Church was not content with myths and legends. Thomas Aquinas, the great theologian of the Middle Ages, spoke officially on behalf of the pope in declaring that although the Jews should not be exterminated, they must be humiliated for the sake of their sins and obstinacy. And by papal briefs and council decrees the people were instructed how to behave toward the Jews.

It is these facts of Church history which have moved the great modern theologian Ad. Harnack to his sharp condemnation of the sin of the modern Church against Israel:

"The heathen Christian church committed an injustice without parallel in history. Emanating from Judaism it wrested from it everything, the divine election, the promises, the prophecies. After robbing her of everything she possessed, the daughter showed her mother the door."

When ministers and monks preached thus about the Jews, early and late, and the general population heard such words pronounced from pulpits, in houses and on the street, they finally had to catch fire. Evil instincts, fanaticism and terror combined with greed to wrench from the Jews their money and debt certificates, issued by the Christians, for loans obtained. It ended in murder and conflagration. And this bloody streak through the history of the Western world has not yet been completely bleached.

True, more moderate and polished words are used in modern language. In Rome the problems were debated by the Ecumenical Council, and the majority of men of the Church have renounced the accusations and prejudice of the past. But the old ghosts have not yet been exorcised. Even today a feeling of animosity surrounds the Jew in Christian countries; he is different, he does not fit in, so many things are whispered about him. The spirit which inspired the painter of the fresco on the church wall continues to cast its shadow. The Jewish enigma stares the Church in the face, uncomprehended and accusing.

Israel and the Church—two contrasts. The Synagogue considers Christian believers in Jesus as deserters. Jews could not and cannot crown an executed man as the Messiah. Even less can they consider him the son of God, because God is the first, and therefore has no father, and He is the last, and consequently has no son. God is one, sacred, indivisible, alone. And the Church maintains that Israel had its day long ago and now belongs to the past.

But superciliousness and over-confidence—no matter on whose part—are signs of fossilization from which no future can grow. Listening only to one's own words, turning a deaf ear to everything the opponent has to say, is an easy escape. If ever that is true, it is true when Jews and Christians meet. The two religions originated from the same source, and no matter how far apart their ways, they are eternally united by delicate bonds, more than they realize, in a secret community of destiny. They can never be rid of one another. Each Christian is two-thirds Jewish, so close is the relationship. The Church will become poor if it stops at the Jew's denial of Christ. For God conceals secrets we cannot comprehend, and paves hidden ways for the people He never abandons.

Have we not all one father?
Hath not one God created us?
Why do we deal treacherously every man against his brother,
Profaning the covenant of our fathers?
                    Malachi 2:10

The Chosen People

David Polish

The doctrine about Israel as God's "Chosen People" is a vexation to many Jews. An examination of the prayerbooks of the Orthodox, Reform, Conservative and Reconstructionist Jews quickly reveals their struggle with the problem.

Sources of the Idea

On Friday night, Jews recite the Kiddush, the prayer of sanctification for the Sabbath, which declares:

> Praised art Thou, Lord our God, Ruler of the universe, who has sanctified us by His commandments and has been gracious to us. His holy Sabbath He has bequeathed to us in love and favor, a reminder of the act of Creation. It is the first of all holy convocations, a reminder of the departure from Egypt. For Thou hast chosen us and sanctified us from among all nations and Thy holy Sabbath Thou hast bequeathed to us in love and favor. Praised art Thou, O Lord, who sanctifiest the Sabbath.

Each morning, and on Sabbaths before reading from the Torah, the following prayer is pronounced:

> Praised art Thou, Lord our God, Ruler of the universe, who has sanctified us from among all nations and hast given us Thy Torah. Praised art Thou, O Lord, the Giver of the Torah.

Toward the end of the daily, Sabbath and festival services, the congregation recites:

> It is our duty to praise the Lord of all things, to ascribe greatness to Him who formed the world in the beginning, that He has not made us like the nations of other lands, and has not placed us like other families of the earth, that He has not made our portion like theirs nor our lot like all their multitude.

On major festivals, the Kiddush, which is similar to the Sabbath Kiddush, includes this addition:

> Thou hast sanctified us from all nations and hast exalted us above all tongues and sanctified us by Thy commandments.

All these prayers clearly express God's special preference for Israel, Israel's separation and distinctiveness from other people, Israel's unique history and destiny, and Israel's elevation above all other nations. That Jews in the Western world are less than comfortable with these declarations is evident in the manner in which they are translated, paraphrased or deleted, either in English or Hebrew, or both.

The Reconstructionist prayerbook, for example, has eliminated all reference, in Hebrew and English, to any suggestion that the Jews are a chosen people. In every passage alluded to above, the text has been radically altered. Thus:

> Thou hast brought us nigh to Thy service and in love and grace hast given us the heritage of Thy holy Sabbath.

The Reform prayerbook is somewhat more ambivalent about the Chosen People concept. In the Kiddush for Sabbath and festivals, in the prayers for reading from the Torah and the prophetic portion, the original Hebrew is retained but the English revised. The Sabbath Kiddush, in a completely new English rendition, exalts only the holiness of the day.

The Conservative prayerbook states: "Who has not made us like the pagans of the world nor placed us like the heathen tribes of the earth." Most enlightening is one of the Orthodox prayerbooks, which, although most deeply rooted in traditional theology, nevertheless takes liberties with the translation, thus:

> It is for us to praise the Lord of all,
> To acclaim the greatness of the God of creation,
> Who has not made us as worldly nations,

Nor set us up as earthly peoples,
Not making our portion as theirs,
Nor our destiny as that of their multitudes.

It might appear that the texts are intended for different audiences, the Hebrew for the faithful, and the English translations for those who cannot accept the original doctrine. It is to be understood, however, as a reflection of an inner conflict which has not been resolved, except in the case of Reconstructionism, which has cut the Gordian knot by rejecting the idea. The lack of congruence between the Hebrew and the English is a dramatic manifestation of a theological dilemma yet to be resolved. Reform theology clings to chosenness in Hebrew but can go only as far as a "calling" in English, while totally rejecting invidious comparisons with the other nations.

The Chosen People concept—like belief in revelation, personal Messiah, resurrection, authority of the Torah—has undergone scrutiny over the ages. This has been done with varying results, depending upon the theological position of the investigators.

Not a Dogma

While the idea of chosenness is prevalent in the Bible, it does not assume the proportions of a dogma, but is rather an inference derived from other factors. Israel is commanded to love God, again and again. It is commanded, by the very act of revelation, to recognize "the Lord your God who brought you out of the land of Egypt." But nowhere is Israel required to believe, as an act of faith or collective acceptance, that it is a chosen people. To be sure, this is affirmed by God or His prophets. There is no escaping that fact.

But this doctrine, if indeed it is a doctrine, differs from others in two respects. Unlike the command to love God, the election principle is challenged in Scripture. It also reflects a serious ambiguity between the popular conception of its meaning and the prophetic conception.

If the doctrine is an embarrassment in contemporary Jewish liturgy, the embarrassment has Biblical roots. Nevertheless, the entire Torah represents a unique relationship between the people Israel and its God. It is the saga of Israel's relationship with God, beginning with the call of Abraham and the promise to his progeny, and continuing with the covenant and all the subsequent events in the history of the people. Other nations are virtually ignored, except as their history intercepts that of Israel. Biblical history is the reaching down by God to use one people, and one people alone, for His purposes.

Meaning of Election

Yet this is only a partial explanation. God's selection of Israel is pervasive and implicit but the specific references to the selection are few and, if examined carefully, qualified and even equivocal. God chooses Israel, as an act of grace on God's part which Israel does not necessarily merit. There is no suggestion of any special qualifications by which the people earns divine favor. The people is warned against arrogating any special merit to itself by a kind of reverse favoritism, a corollary of which turns up in the prophecy of Amos.

In Deuteronomy 7:7, the people is specifically admonished that its selection is due not to any inherent grandeur but precisely because of its lowly state. The Chosen People nowhere means the "superior people," an error to which friends and enemies, Jews and Christians, have fallen victim. Yet there is not a shred of evidence in Scripture suggesting that Israel was regarded as unusually endowed. Quite the contrary: "My father (Jacob) was a wandering Aramean." The Passover Haggadah accentuates the less than noble origins of Israel by adding, "At first our ancestors were idol worshippers." Scripture details how God brings a band of dispirited and cantankerous slaves out of Egypt.

It is both a rebellious people and one marked still by the scars of oppression. But it is also a people which has experienced redemption and revelation.

What then is there in the people that despite its smallness, its paucity among the nations of the world, its lowly state, marks it for divine selection?

Both the concept and the term "selection" (*Bechirah*) are not limited to Israel. In the technical sense in which the word is used, it is also applied to places, institutions, religious practices and classes. Jerusalem is "chosen" as the place which God desires. The Temple is "chosen" as the place where God's spirit is to dwell.

But most suggestive is God's selection of the priests. "For the Lord thy God has chosen him out of all thy tribes, to stand to minister in the name of the Lord, him and his sons for ever" (Deuteronomy 18:5). A few verses later, the function of the selected group is spelled out—to serve God: "And the priests and sons of Levi shall come near—for them the Lord thy God has chosen to minister to Him, and to bless in the name of the Lord; and according to their word shall every controversy and every stroke be" (21:5).

In its covenant relationship with God, Israel is identified as a priestly community: "You shall be a kingdom of priests and a holy people." The specialized function of one tribe becomes generalized and is applied to the entire people. The function of the people becomes a universal mission "to be a light to the nations, to open the eyes of the blind, to set the prisoner free" (Isaiah 42:7, 8). By analogy, the chosenness of Israel is related to the fulfillment of certain priestly functions. This is stated specifically in Deuteronomy 7:6.*

Selection and Redemption

Aside from the *nature* of the selection, we are still puzzled by the *reason* for the selection. Why was this lowly people singled out for a special place in the divine plan?

When the Ten Commandments are proclaimed at Sinai, God identifies Himself to Israel as the Redeemer of the enslaved: "I am the Lord your God who brought you out of the land of Egypt, out of the house of bondage." He does not proclaim Himself as the Creator of the universe, an aspect of divinity which is shared with all humanity. The self-disclosure to Israel alone is predicated on its redemption from Egypt. In nearly every citation dealing with Israel's chosenness, the selection is rooted either in the initial redemption or in a future redemption from suffering which is to recapitulate the release from Egyptian enslavement.

Why does the text say again and again that Israel has been chosen "from among all the nations"? Because, as the text itself indicates, Israel alone was taken out of bondage by God. Why does Israel alone merit this particular historical and divine consideration? The Torah does not deal with any history other than that of Israel, and the rest of Scripture is equally silent. Even the covenant with Abraham, who from the very first is singled out by God from among all other men, is based solidly on a future event—the enslavement of his descendants and their divine rescue. Written as it was *after* the event, it reflects a keen concern with establishing a relationship between selection and redemption. Thus, God's act is not entirely one of inexplicable grace, but has a firm foundation in an historical event into which God enters.

When Israel fell upon difficult times, it was reminded of its selection by God who would, the prophet foretold, repeat the first redemption. Indeed, the Exodus becomes the paradigm for all subsequent redemptions of Israel.

Even Balaam, a heathen and no friend of Israel, becomes possessed by the awareness of Israel's intimacy with "the God who brought them out of Egypt" (Numbers 23:21, 22).

*The classic references to selection in the Torah are to be found in Deuteronomy 4:37; 7:7; 10:15; 14:2.

A second concept derives from this redemptive aspect of selection. It is apprehended in Balaam's discourse when he says, "For from the top of the rock I see him, and from the hills I behold him. It is a people that shall dwell alone, and shall not be reckoned among the nations" (Numbers 23:9). Awareness of Israel's unique place in history, its differentiation from other nations, is clearly discerned. This, too, is a factor which has contemporary relevance.

Just as selection is bound up with redemption so too is it bound up with the derivative of redemption—the Torah, the third category of the essence of selection. Every Deuteronomic passage referring to the selection admonishes Israel to be faithful to the commandments. Israel is *the* people of Torah. Historically, it is chosen because it is released from captivity. Morally, its consequent obligation is to preserve the Torah. This is stated almost syllogistically in Deuteronomy 7:6-11:

> For thou art a holy people unto the Lord thy God: the Lord thy God hath chosen thee to be His own treasure, out of all peoples that are upon the face of the earth. The Lord did not set His love upon you, nor choose you, because ye were more in number than any people—for ye were the fewest of all peoples—but because the Lord loved you, and because He would keep the oath which He swore unto your fathers, hath the Lord brought you out with a mighty hand, and redeemed you out of the house of bondage, from the hand of Pharaoh king of Egypt. Know therefore that the Lord thy God, He is God; the faithful God, who keepeth covenant and mercy with them that love Him and keep His commandments to a thousand generations; and repayeth them that hate Him to their face, to destroy them; He will not be slack to him that hateth Him, He will repay him to his face. Thou shalt therefore keep the commandment, and the statutes, and the ordinances, which I command thee this day, to do them.

Selection and Covenant

The covenant is the culminating act in the divine-historical process. It is the marriage, as it were, of God and Israel, and it is indissoluble. Israel may be punished severely. It may be brought to the very gate of annihilation, but the covenant itself is indissoluble, and through it the people is renewed.

In the post-Biblical period, the historical aspect, centered in Israel's past deliverance, took on special urgency, particularly during the Jewish people's medieval agony. In the writings of

Yehudah Halevi Israel's selection *and* superiority assumed massive proportions. Selection was linked to two factors—the psychological need for justification induced by anti-Jewish oppression, and the futuristic hope, shading off into eschatological expectations, of the Messianic advent. In addition, while Israel yearned for redemption, its sensitivity to the living fact that it alone was the people of the Torah took on special intensity. In the tenth century, Saadia, the Jewish philosopher-theologian, wrote, "Our people is a people only through its Torah."

It is clearly presumptuous for any people or religious community to lay claim to God's exclusive concern. This may explain why Maimonides chose not to make the selection of Israel a fourteenth article of the faith. But this is not to deny that the concept has contemporary relevance. Whatever purpose God may have for the nations and the faiths, Israel appears to have been selected to endure *as Israel.* A compelling fact of our time is the very existence of the Jewish people, a wonder of history that must be confronted at every turn.

Biblical insight caught the remarkable link between redemption and selection, which applies today with special clarity to the condition of the people Israel. With Amos, we assert that Israel is not the only people that has been brought out of the pit, but Israel is in fact the only people whose entire career has been a fluctuation between annihilation and renewal, destruction and resurrection, death and transfiguration. Judaism has seen this ebb and flow in our fortunes as a continuous recapitulation of the original slavery and deliverance. Every exile has been Egypt. Every tyrant has been Pharaoh. Every deliverance has been the first redemption enlarged.

Greater in the dimension of space, greater in time, greater in terror and agony even than Egypt has been the oppression of Israel in Europe, culminating in the Nazi period. The sheer fact of survival under conditions of relentless assault, even if Israel were nothing but a nomadic pack for 3500 years, would in itself be cause for wonder. But it has not been survival alone, but a series of periodic confrontations with evil.

The capacity of Israel to stand at the crossroads of history and by its own witness attest to its indestructibility in the face of overwhelming evil is an unassailable fact. This is divine selection.

But there is also demonic selection. During the Second World War, Hitler's agents went all over Nazi Europe to make what they called "selections" of Jews for transport to the death camps. These selections, then and even before, represented the resistance and defiance of the demonic in history. Freud has annotated the specific selection of the Jews for oppression as a rejection by the oppressor of the God whom the Jew represented and, even more, the God who entered into the Christian world from Judaism.

Israel has endured, in the words of Balaam, because "it is a people that dwells alone and is not reckoned as are other nations." It is defiant of the deterministic rules of history which insist that every civilization undergoes a process of rise, decline and death. It has followed its own solitary course, living both among the nations and preserving its own spirit.

Israel's Special Experience

Moreover, no other people has undergone the unique metamorphosis which Israel experiences today—to be a people which is both sovereign in the State of Israel, and at the same time part of a world community beyond the confines of that state. It is a metamorphosis, yet a return to a prior condition when Israel enjoyed both autonomy and a Diaspora existence before Rome overwhelmed Palestine. This is more than a unique historical phenomenon. It is an illustration to the world of the dynamic possibilities of nationhood and universal commitment within our world order where growing disenchantment with nationalism summons the peoples of our globe to a higher goal than parochial patriotism.

Finally, Israel is the people of Torah. No matter how widely Jews within Judaism may differ, they all cling to Torah as a central, indispensable aspect of Jewish life. Significantly and perhaps as a consequence of Israel's martyrdom, Torah is exerting an increasing pull back toward the center. Less and less is it being treated, even in radical circles, as an antiquarian, analysis-ridden document, and increasingly as the source of Jewish commitment and direction. Whether a Jew believes in literal revelation or not, Jews can declare with conviction that Israel's orbit in human and sacred history is governed by adherence to the authority of the Torah.

The crucial question is: who selects, God or Israel? Is this a divine appointment or a self-appointment? One thing we know: Israel did not take upon itself the yoke of Judaism and the yoke of martyrdom in order to perpetuate a wilful fraud on itself. But could it have been deluded? There are some who believe this. But there are others who believe that the living God manifests Himself in history, by events which cannot be subjected merely to inter-disciplinary scrutiny. Such an event is Israel, which ultimately makes its claim by reciting: "I shall not die but live and declare the acts of God."

Covenants--Old and New

Seymour Siegel

B'rit or covenant is a word which occurs over and over again in Jewish religious language. The young Jewish male is inducted into the people of Israel through a ceremony known as *b'rit*. The Sabbath is called *Ot B'rit,* sign of the covenant. The Ten Commandments were inscribed on the *luhot ha-brit,* tablets of the covenant. And the largest Jewish fraternal and service order is called B'nai B'rith—children of the covenant.

"Never imagine you have rightly grasped a Biblical idea," the theologian Paul Ramsey says, "until you have reduced it to a corollary of the idea of the covenant." That idea conveys the notion of agreement or pact, which, according to the Biblical view, the people of Israel made with the Almighty.

> Now, therefore if ye will obey My voice indeed, and keep My covenant, then ye shall be a peculiar treasure unto Me above all people: And ye shall be unto Me a kingdom of priests and a holy nation (Exodus 19:5-6).

The sons of Israel were not to be a people like all other peoples. Its existence was not to be like that of other nations. The people had a special vocation, a specific purpose, a particular duty: to be the representatives of God in the world. The obligations of the covenant were outlined in the Torah and the tradition. There were visible signs of the covenant—placed on the flesh of every male (through circumcision), and observed every seventh day (through the Sabbath) and on the festivals and holy days of the calendar.

New Covenant vs. Old Covenant

It was around the idea of covenant that the people of Israel could make sense of their communal life and find the strength to live that life. Once the idea of covenant was questioned, the whole structure of Jewish self-understanding was in danger.

The most powerful challenge to Israel's view of its destiny came from Christianity. The new religion readily acknowledged that God had once made a covenant with the children of Abraham, Isaac and Jacob. Indeed, this concept was at the basis of the Christian assertion and interpretation of history. But, according to Christian teachers, the old covenant had been abrogated and replaced by a new covenant or new testament. Through union with Jesus, the Gentile became part of that new covenant, the New Israel, which replaced the old Israel.

"So, remember," Paul tells recent Gentile converts to Christianity, "that at that time when you were without Christ you were aliens to the commonwealth of Israel, and strangers to the covenant of promise . . . but now, through your union with Jesus Christ, you who were once far away, have been brought near so that you are no longer strangers and foreigners, but fellow citizens of God's people and of the family of God" (Ephesians 2:12-19).

It is true that Paul himself is not so certain that the new covenant has replaced the "old one." In Letters to the Romans, he says: "And thou [speaking to the Gentiles], being a wild olive tree, wert grafted in among them [that is, the Jews], and with them partakest of the root and fatness of the olive tree."

But later Christians were adamant in asserting that Christianity was the legitimate heir of the *b'rit*—thus making Judaism, the so-called "old" covenant, superfluous. Jesus, who was seen as the Messiah, was Israel personified. Through union with him, the believer became an heir of Israel's covenant. The Law, the Torah, the commandments were no longer necessary. The new covenant required faith in Jesus and adherence to the church. It did not require observance of the Torah.

If Christianity's claim were true, there was no reason for the Jewish people to continue to exist. The new covenant had superseded the Law of the "old" covenant, and the Christian Church was the heir of Abraham, Isaac and Jacob.

Jews, of course, could not take this claim seriously. They saw no reason even to engage in serious argument. To them the covenant was eternal; only at the end of days, when the real Messiah would come, would there be a "new" covenant written on the hearts of men. By no stretch of the imagination could the claim of the new Church be accepted.

Christianity presented no theological problem to Jews, who knew that men had and would have different religions. They were bound by the seven Noahide laws, which, if fulfilled, gave them a share in the world to come. The *b'rit* continued to define the purpose and essence of *Jewish* existence.

For Christians, Judaism represented a very serious theological problem. If Christianity were true, there was no reason for Jews to continue to exist and observe their religion. When the Jews refused to accept the Christian belief that the old covenant had been replaced by the new one, they became objects of hatred and abuse. They were seen as stubborn and blind, and their religion was despised and denigrated.

The issue was drawn: Who are the real Jews—the heirs of the covenant—the children of Abraham, Isaac and Jacob, or the new Christians? When Jews made it clear that they could see no reason to believe that their covenant had outlived its force, Christians initiated the lamentable and tragic history of the "Jewish-Christian" argument. The triumphant Church refused to acknowledge Judaism as a legitimate and honorable religion, and Jews became objects of hatred, persecution and (in the words of the late Jules Isaac) the victims of the teaching of contempt.

One other strategy was sought. Christianity undertook to missionize the Jews. Sometimes these efforts were carried on with kindness, but all too often more drastic methods were used.

The Schema

This argument about covenants—old and new—has defined the Jewish-Christian relationship even to our own day. The Schema on the Jews adopted at Vatican II speaks very warmly of the Jews. But it also states:

> The Church, therefore, cannot forget that she received the revelation of the Old Testament through the people with whom God in his inexpressible mercy deigned to establish the Ancient Covenant. . . . As Holy Scripture testifies, Jerusalem did not recognize the time of her visitation nor did the Jews in large number accept the gospel; indeed not a few opposed the spreading of it. Nevertheless, according to the Apostle, the Jew remains most dear to God *because of their fathers* [italics mine].

In other words, Jews should be viewed with affection because they originally received the promises. But there is no statement in the Schema affirming that Judaism today is a legitimate,

. valid spiritual body. Jews are still the objects of missionizing and still the adherents of a religion which once was valid but is not so today.

Never before, since the beginning of our era, have the opportunities for Jewish-Christian dialogue and discussion been as hopeful as today. The destruction of European Jewry, the new ecumenical spirit and the challenge of un-religion to all faith systems have made it possible to renew discussions with candor and to work for understanding which may help overcome the tragic history of past centuries. But no true dialogue between Judaism and Christianity can be carried on unless Judaism is recognized by Christianity to be legitimate, and all attempts to absorb Judaism into Christianity be eschewed.

Somehow, the problem of the covenants—old and new— will have to be solved. How can the two religions live together in theological harmony? Is there some way in which one can affirm the truth of his own religion and not negate, at the same time, the integrity of his neighbor's faith?

A Helpful Approach

A growing number of thinkers—Jewish and Christian—have felt that the way to a solution has been pointed out by Franz Rosenzweig, the great German-Jewish theologian. Rosenzweig takes Christianity seriously:

> Our recognition of Christianity rests, in fact, upon Christianity, namely upon the fact that Christianity recognizes us. It is the Torah, ultimately, which is spread abroad by Bible societies to the most distant islands . . . No one *comes* to the Father—except through him [e.g., Jesus]. No one *comes* . . . but the situation is different when one need no longer come to the Father because he *is* already with him. That is the case of the nation of Israel.

Rosenzweig is saying that there may very well be a new covenant or testament in addition to the "old" one. But this new one, Christianity, does not cancel out the old one; its function is instead to make it possible for the nations of the world to enter into the Israelite covenant. There are two covenants: one with the people of Israel, which is Judaism; the other with the Gentiles or the nations of the world, through Christianity. Through Judaism, the individual Jew finds his way to God. Through Christianity, the *goyim*, the nations, establish their relationship to the Almighty. Christianity is the Judaism of the Gentiles. The "new" testament supplements the "old" covenant. Both are parallel lines meeting in eternity.

If this suggestion were to be accepted by Jew and Christian, it would be possible to open a new era of dialogue and mutual enlightenment. Christians would not denigrate Judaism by viewing it as a vestige, an anachronism of ancient times. They would cease their missionizing activities vis-a-vis Jews. For Jews, there would be a new recognition of the importance of Christianity, of its spiritual dimension and its task to bring the word of God to the far islands.

Need for True Dialogue

True dialogue is the need of the hour. But it cannot take place until Christians cease seeing Judaism as a superannuated blind community and until Jews understand the meaning of Christianity. Franz Rosenzweig points the way to such a mutual understanding and esteem. Christianity does not supersede Judaism but is the way in which the Gentiles come to God. Judaism is not the result of blindness but is the content of the covenant of the children of Israel, who are God's people.

It is encouraging to see that important Christian voices are being raised in support of this point of view. Professor A. Roy Eckhardt of Lehigh University has written in *Christianity and the Children of Israel:*

> The missionary view is . . . challenged [not only by liberalism but also] by some who accept Christian faith as in a certain sense final. . . What is usually involved here is the contention that the Jews have a unique function in the divine economy. . . That claim [that if the mission to the Jews is abandoned] it logically follows that missionary endeavor has to cease for all people is seen as failing to realize that Judaism and other religions are not on the same plane. Christianity and Judaism have a relationship lacking between Christianity and other religion. . . . I have no interest in trying to convert the Jews to Christianity.

A new turn in the dispute about covenants—old and new—will have to precede genuine conversation between Jew and Christian. The Christian treatment of the Jew has been one of the gravest accusations which history can make against religion; Jews demand recognition of past sins and the determination not to repeat them.

Christianity and Judaism are two ways, both directed toward the divine. They are communities with different memories and different histories. But even in the face of these differences we can walk together in harmony and unity.

Needed Areas
of Understanding

Robert Gordis

The events of the past decades, both in Germany and in the United States, have demonstrated that the cultivation of "good will" is not enough in an age of crisis. To be sure, a friendly personal attitude toward men of different religious and racial backgrounds is highly praiseworthy. But if it is purely emotional, it is not likely to survive the buffetings of adverse circumstance or the strains of group tensions.

What is required is an intellectual and moral base for good will, rooted in the conscious recognition of the right of all men to be different. A virile spirit of brotherhood and mutual regard between Christians and Jews must rest upon an understanding by each of the content and spirit of the religio-ethical traditions of the other. Moreover, the conventional "interfaith" stress upon "the things that unite us," genuine though they be, bypasses all the elements of divergence which are the breeding grounds of ill will and prejudice and supply the rationale for discrimination and persecution.

It must be confessed, however, that the importance of the Jewish attitude toward Christianity is primarily theoretical. Since Jews constitute a minority group everywhere in the world except in the State of Israel—and even there they are conscious of being a tiny island in an Arab sea—they do not possess either the power or the influence to be determining factors in the destiny of twentieth-century man. By and large, Jews are far more likely to be on the receiving end than on the dispensing end of ill will and prejudice. This does not, of course, imply that Jews are free from the moral and intellectual obligation to understand the content of Christianity and its basic concerns.

On the other hand, the Christian has an obligation to strive after an understanding of Jews and Judaism not only for moral reasons, but on compelling practical grounds—because it is a matter of life or death for the Jewish people. There is a categorical imperative for Christians to seek to penetrate to the genuine spirit and content of Judaism and to the innermost attitudes and emotions of their Jewish fellow citizens, precisely because the majority has the power to work its will upon the minority. Judaism impinges upon the life and thought of the modern world in at least four related yet distinct areas, each of which needs to be delimited and taken into account.

1. *For its own sake, Christianity must maintain and deepen its understanding and attachment to the Hebrew Scriptures.*

This should include not merely a familiarity with the text and content of the Old Testament but a knowledge of the three-thousand-year-old tradition of Biblical interpretation in Judaism as well. This is desirable for laymen; for teachers of religion it is indispensable. Today it is clear that Marcionism in any form, which denies the sanctity and authority of the Old Testament, leads to a fatal distortion of the Christian message and that a Christianity cut loose from its roots in the Hebrew Scriptures has neither strength nor staying power. When the early Church stigmatized Marcionism as a heresy in the second century, it revealed its essential healthy-mindedness. In our day the bloody neo-Marcionism of Aryan Christianity in Nazi Germany has demonstrated that the attempt to divorce the Christian world view from the Hebrew Scriptures is a heresy that is finally expiated in blood.

Moreover, what is needed is the full Old Testament, not an expurgated or abridged selection. Scholars like Professor W. D. Davies have pointed out that modern scholarship understands that the Biblical heritage of Christianity is not restricted to the prophets of Israel but must include the Law, which tended to be downgraded in Christian circles.

We may go a step further. The Hebrew canon recognizes three sections in the Hebrew Scriptures. By the side of the Torah and the Prophets, the Bible contains the Hagiographa, which enshrines the products of Biblical wisdom. How much religious depth would Christianity lose without the Psalms and how much narrower would its intellectual horizons be without the books of Proverbs, Job, and Ecclesiastes! It is the totality of the Hebrew Scriptures which cries out for understanding and use by the teachers and expounders of Christianity.

In addition, there is a quest today for new insight into the deeper implications of the Biblical text for modern man. This is evident in the pages of Kierkegaard, Rosenzweig, Tillich, Buber, Niebuhr, Heschel and many other thinkers. This enterprise has much to gain from contact with the religio-ethical interpretation of the Bible to be found in the vast expanses of the Talmud and Midrashic literature.

Modern Christian scholars who rediscover the treasures of Jewish Biblical scholarship will be reviving an honorable Christian tradition. It goes back to such Church Fathers as Origen, who in his stupendous *Hexapla* collated all the extant Greek versions of the Hebrew Bible with the Hebrew text, and Jerome, whose Vulgate was a massive effort to discover the *Hebraica veritas* for the good of the Church. Both scholars frequently consulted Jewish teachers and cited views of rabbinic exegesis. This tradition of scholarly collaboration continued, though with interruptions, through the Middle Ages.

Luther leaned heavily upon the Latin Commentaries of Nicholas de Lyra, which were largely an epitome of the medieval Jewish commentator, Rashi. As a result, Luther's classic translation of the Bible into German has been described, with some exaggeration, as a German version of Rashi. On the other hand, the English Authorized Version of 1611 drew primarily upon Rabbi David Kimhi. These commentators and other great Jewish medieval scholars still possess rich treasures that are often overlooked—to our loss.

Moreover, Jewish Biblical interpretation has continued uninterrupted to the present day. When this rich quarry is ignored, as Catholic exegesis was wont to be ignored until recently in Protestant circles and as American scholarship still tends to be overlooked overseas, the level of our common understanding of Holy Writ is gravely impoverished. Fortunately, the ecumenical spirit is making itself increasingly felt in various cooperative scholarly undertakings.

2. *A knowledge of Judaism is essential to Christians for an understanding of the background of Jesus, the Apostles, Paul and the early Church.*

There should be no need to labor the point that it was not Biblical religion but Rabbinical Judaism which nurtured the human career of Jesus. We may delimit his environment still further as being basically Pharisaic Judaism. Jesus shared the same Pharisaic attitudes and beliefs which were accepted among virtually all Jews in his day, with the exception of the Sadducees. All the other sects, the Essenes, the Zealots and the Apocalyptists, represented extreme formulations of one or another element in Pharisaic teaching.

Such basic elements of faith as the resurrection of the dead, the Messiah and the Kingdom of God, the primacy of the two commandments to love God and one's neighbor, without which Christianity is inconceivable, were all Pharisaic doctrines. The massive commentary on the New Testament by Strack-Billerbeck, as well as the writings of countless other scholars, have indicated hundreds of points of contact between the earliest Christian circles of Jesus, his disciples and followers, and Rabbinic Judaism. When Paul, whose Diaspora background was radically different from that of the Palestinian Jesus, described himself as "a Pharisee, son of a Pharisee" (Acts 23:6), he was underscoring the truth that it was Rabbinic Judaism—modified, to be sure, in different circles and varying countries—which was the universal spiritual climate of world Jewry and the soil from which Christianity sprang.

The discovery of the Dead Sea Scrolls and the elucidation of their contents have wrought a veritable revolution in our understanding of the sources of Christianity. In the past it was generally believed that by and large the faith and ethical teaching of Christianity were Jewish in origin, while the theology and ritual of the Church represented the influence of Hellenism and Oriental religion. This attitude was supported by the fact that parallels between Jewish rabbinic sources and the New Testament were most plentiful for the Synoptic Gospels and much rarer for the Gospel of John and the Pauline Epistles.

Today much of the content of early Christian thought and practice that was previously thought to have its source in extra-Jewish circles, whether in Hellenistic thought or in the mystery religions, is now seen to emanate from the life and outlook of the Dead Sea Sectarians. It is true that the Dead Sea Scrolls show many affinities of content and expression with the Fourth Gospel and the Epistles. Such elements as the boundless faith in the Righteous Teacher, the ideals of celibacy and of property held in common, the emphasis upon purity, the conflict between "the children of light" and "the children of darkness," the Messianic interpretation of Scriptural passages, the communion meal of the faithful, which is a prototype of the Messianic banquet at "the end of days"—all these features of the early Christian Church are represented in Jewish documents.

It has now become clear that much of the assumed Gentile influence on early Christianity is not Gentile at all. The Christian debt to Judaism becomes immeasurably enlarged, for it now includes both the mainstream of normative Judaism and the lesser currents of Jewish sectarianism.

In describing Christianity as the offspring of Judaism we are not denying or minimizing its own individuality. In order to explore the nature of this complex relationship to Judaism and reveal the unique character of the Christian vision, one requires a knowledge of Judaism from within, as well as of Christian life and thought. The student and teacher of Christianity requires some firsthand knowledge of the great literary documents of normative Judaism: the Mishnah, the Talmud, and the Midrash, which are indispensable for a full understanding of the origins and development of Christianity. Fortunately these original sources, as well as a reliable scholarly literature dealing with them, are today available in English and other modern languages.

3. *The Christian world must strive to divest itself of the vestiges of theological animus, often decked out in "scientific" garb. Jews and Judaism must be recognized as living elements of the modern world and not as a "fossilized relic of Syriac society."*

Toynbee's famous and unfortunate phrase was a secularized version of a widespread religious theory. According to this view, Jews are members of a petrified community, which for two thousand years since the advent of Christianity has shriveled up and lost all its positive attributes except that of being a stiff-necked people.

In spite of the hoary antiquity of this doctrine born of religious controversy centuries ago, it may be suggested that its retention is not essential to Christian loyalty and vitality. There is sufficient creative capacity within Christian theology to evolve a conception of the role of the Jewish people in the Christian world that will be both truer and kinder. This revision of outlook needs to begin with Christian scholars and teachers, but it must reach the "grass roots" in the pew and the classroom and ultimately affect "the man in the street." For modern Judaism is not the vestigial remains of Old Testament religion, though obviously rooted in it. To describe Judaism in terms of the Old Testament is as misleading as would be a picture of contemporary American life derived solely from the Constitution.

Modern Judaism is the product of a long and rich development of Biblical thought. It possesses a normative tradition embodied in the Mishnah and the Talmud, as well as in the Responsa and the Codes of the post-Talmudic period, which continue to enrich its content to the present day.

Nor is this all. By the side of the dominant strands in normative Judaism are the aberrant tendencies, sectarian and heretical, that were never without influence and cannot be ignored. The various schools, conventionally subsumed under the headings of Orthodoxy, Conservatism and Reform, do not begin to exhaust the variety of religious experience and attitude to be found in the Jewish community. In brief, modern Judaism in all its forms is not Biblical Judaism, not even Talmudic Judaism, nor even medieval Judaism, but the resultant of all three, modified, enriched and challenged by two thousand years of Western civilization.

Some Christian thinkers who have penetrated to the spirit of the Jewish tradition have discovered within it resources that can enrich the content of the Christian world view and help us meet some of the massive problems confronting the free society of the West and the international community of tomorrow. In such areas as sex, personal morality and the family, nationalism and the international community, the relationship of religious loyalty and freedom of conscience, the authentic Jewish tradition has insights and attitudes of value not only to its devotees but to all men.

While public religious debates are now a thing of the past, the effort to demonstrate the alleged ethical superiority of Christianity over Judaism continues to be a problem. The well-worn and threadbare contrast still continues to be drawn between the Old Testament "God of justice" and "the God of love" of the New Testament. Every competent scholar, Christian and Jewish alike, knows that the Old Testament conceived of God in terms of love as well as of justice, just as Jesus' God manifested Himself in justice as well as in love, for justice without love is cruelty and love without justice is caprice.

Nevertheless the practice still goes on, in the pulpit and in popular publications, of contrasting the primitivism, tribalism and legalism of the Old Testament with the spirituality, universalism and freedom of the New, to the manifest disadvantage of the former.

Another widespread practice which should be surrendered is that of referring to the Old Testament verses quoted in the New as original New Testament passages. The Golden Rule continues to be cited from the New Testament, when the fact is that, like any Jewish teacher, Jesus was citing the Hebrew Scriptures as did Paul.

4. *The fourth area where there is a burning need for greater understanding on the part of both the clergy and laity is the character and outlook of contemporary Jewry.*

Today priests, ministers and rabbis are being brought into contact during their college and seminary training with politics, economics, sociology, psychology, as well as the natural sciences. It is increasingly recognized that unless the insights of religion are related to these fields they will remain suspended in mid-air, and, having no grip upon the human conscience, will exert no practical effect upon human conduct. The parish minister and priest, the church administrator and religious educator will serve the needs of a pluralistic society of equals more truly if their background will include a comprehension of the lives and institutions, the groups and divisions, the problems and the goals of their Jewish neighbors.

In one sense, this call for an apparently secular approach to contemporary Jewry is of greater practical moment than the modern traditional theological approach we have previously urged. Modern Jews are profoundly aware and deeply appreciative of the vast reservoir of good will to be found among their Christian friends and neighbors. They know them as generally humane and compassionate, fair-minded and tolerant in their individual relationships; and allowing for the weaknesses of human nature, Jews attempt to reciprocate.

However, it must be confessed that most Jews do not see the same virtues in evidence in the Christian community viewed as a collective entity. However paradoxical it may seem, it is almost as though men's actions were better than their professions! There is far too much evidence in the history and etiology of anti-Semitism that seems to support the view that Christian men and women display good will because they are human and exhibit prejudice because they are Christian.

The two major events of modern Jewish history, the Nazi holocaust and the establishment of the State of Israel, underscore the reasons for this feeling. Jews recognize that there is genuine contrition in many Christian religious circles for the extermination of six million Jewish men, women and children. Jews are also realistic enough to realize that the horrors of the crematoria and the gas chambers cannot loom as large for Christians as for Jews. Though their emotions are deeply involved, Jews are increasingly recognizing that they must try to forgive what they cannot forget and try to forget what they cannot forgive. But the wounds are deep and the scar tissue takes time to form.

Jews are also deeply appreciative of the warm sympathy of many distinguished religious leaders. Thus Professor Amos N. Wilder speaks of "the deep reappraisal into which all Christians *must have been shocked* by the mass persecutions of the recent period." * But Jews wonder how widely the rank and file of Christians share the sense of contrition which he and other sensitive leaders, Catholic and Protestant alike, have expressed. In a poll conducted by the University of California, close to half the Americans polled agreed with the statement that "Jews should stop complaining about what happened to them in Nazi Germany."

*Italics ours.

The State of Israel, which is part of the pulsating present, is another major event where the Christian attitude is often disappointing to Jews. It cannot be too strongly emphasized that virtually all Jews who feel any sense of attachment to their heritage are profoundly dedicated to the State of Israel as their spiritual center and a major refuge for their oppressed brethren. If "home" may be defined as "the place they must let you in when you knock," the land of Israel is the homeland of world Jewry in no political sense but in spiritual terms.

The truly unique nature of the Jewish group, best described by the Biblical term *am*, "people," is the key to understanding the special relationship of Jews to the land of Israel. Everywhere in the free world Jews are deeply committed to the lands of their sojourning and are thoroughly integrated into the political, economic and cultural life of their native or adopted fatherlands. Nevertheless they harbor a love for that little corner of the earth's surface where their people had its origin, where their tradition was born, where their brothers are masters of their own destiny, where their cultural and spiritual heritage can grow without let or hindrance.

Since the State of Israel is not only an objective reality but an essential element in the world view of most Jews, any true understanding of contemporary Jewry must seek to include the State of Israel. What is desired—and desirable—is not that the Christian Church become a partisan of the State of Israel, or that it undertake to defend its every act and attitude. Jews themselves, both in Israel and throughout the world, have not hesitated to criticize many aspects of Israeli life. But what Jews would like to see is a growing recognition by Christians of the legitimacy of Jewish rights in Palestine which, incidentally, does not and need not imply any denial of the legitimate rights of the Arabs. The State of Israel must be seen against the background of the Jewish tragedy in the twentieth century —the Nazi holocaust in the recent past, and the barring of the gates against the admission of Jews in many lands of the democratic West and their persecution in the Communist East. Far too many well-intentioned members of the Christian community have yet to recognize that even now the State of Israel represents literally the only asylum of life and hope for untold numbers of oppressed Jews the world over.

It should not be difficult for believing Christians who cherish the Bible to reject the falsehood that the Jews who return to Israel are lackeys of capitalist imperialism, as Communist propaganda asserts, or the agents of Western colonialism, as the Arab dictators and monarchs proclaim. The Jewish settlers in the State of Israel are members of an ancient people who,

as in the days of Ezra and Nehemiah, are striving to restore
their national life in its ancestral home. Though driven from
Palestine by force of arms, they have continued to pray and
aspire for their restoration for nineteen hundred years of exile,
and have never abdicated their historic claim to the Promised
Land, enunciated in the pages of the Bible.

This last consideration should carry weight with Christians
who revere the Scripture as the word of God. Dr. Chaim Weiz-
mann was once asked at a British Royal Commission hearing
what the basis of the Jewish title to Palestine was. He answered, "Gentlemen, you are under the impression that the
mandate is our Bible. The truth is that the Bible is our
mandate."

No More Missionizing

There is one more tension area which must concern all who
are sincerely interested in furthering the dialogue of Christianity and Judaism. This is the long-standing practice of Christian
missionary activity among Jews. The traditional Christian
doctrine was expressed by the International Committee on the
Christian Approach to the Jews at its conference in 1931:
"Judaism is as much without Christ as Mohammedanism and
Hinduism, Buddhism and Confucianism. Either all people need
Christ or none."

Jews have always been hurt by the assumption of superiority which underlies the widespread efforts being made to convert them to Christianity. Today this assumption is resented
by all other non-Christians as well, Mohammedans, Hindus,
Buddhists and Confucianists. Each of these traditions is able
to demonstrate, to the satisfaction of its own communicants
at least, that it possesses adequate resources for the spiritual
and ethical life of its devotees.

It will be recalled that in one of the earlier drafts of the
proposed Schema on the Jews at the Second Vatican Council,
the Christian duty of practicing kindness to Jews was closely
linked to the Christian hope for the conversion of the Jews. It
aroused a storm of protest not only within the Jewish community but among many leaders of the Roman Catholic Church
and untold Catholic laymen, who did not abate a jot or tittle
of their loyalty to their church but who understood and honored the sincerity of Jews' loyalty to Judaism. Fortunately this
ill-considered addendum was muted in the final draft and the
call for fairness and friendship to the Jewish people was not
linked to ulterior considerations.

Modern Jews understand that through the centuries Chris-

tians have expressed their love for their fellow men by striving
to bring them within the pale of Christian belief. On the other
hand, Christians should understand that Jews are no less sincere in their love for their fellow men. However, Judaism believes that "salvation" is not exclusively "of the Jews." Because
of the rabbinic teaching that "the righteous of all nations have
their share in the world to come," Judaism accords to all men
the right to preserve their own religious tradition and group
individuality.

Can Christianity be asked to abandon its hope of converting
Jews to the Gospel? A few Christian thinkers, like Reinhold
Niebuhr, have not hesitated to answer this question in the
affirmative, though most Christian teachers would probably
not agree. Increasingly, there is a growing emphasis in Christian circles not upon missionary activity directed toward the
Jews but, in Professor Wilder's words, upon a witness to Christian truth which "will take the form either of silent deeds of
justice and goodness or of dialogue without ulterior motives."

Christians are not called upon to abandon their hope for a
world converted to the Gospels, any more than traditional
Judaism has given up the prophetic faith that the day will
come when "the Lord shall be one and His name one." If the
election of Israel, which is basic to the Christian claim, has
any meaning, it must be that men must leave to God the
achievement of His purpose through and with His people at
"the end of days." Men must learn to express their hopes in a
spirit of humility, always conscious that His thoughts are not
our thoughts and His ways are not our ways.

To urge a modification of the Christian attitude and practice
on missionary activity is not as radical a proposal as may at
first sight appear. The history both of Christianity and of Judaism, and indeed of every living tradition, offers countless instances of doctrines as well as practices that were important
at one period and then have receded into the background,
sometimes to be revived in a subsequent age.

It should therefore be possible for Christians to recognize
that genuine conversion can come only through the grace of
God and in His own time, and that the life of dialogue, which
means talking together and living together, should not be viti-
ated by the hope of utilizing these contacts for missionary
activities.

Crucial Areas

The Nazi holocaust, the State of Israel and the Christian
missionary tradition constitute three areas of profound con-

cern to Jews who wish to love and respect their brothers and hope to be respected and loved by them. The Christian community of today and tomorrow needs to be led to a sympathetic understanding of Jewish attitudes and feelings on these crucial subjects.

According to Hasidic tradition, the great saint, Rabbi Levi Yitzhak of Berdichev, was wont to say that he had learned the meaning of love from a drunken peasant. One day he had occasion to come into an inn, in the corner of which two peasants were sitting over their liquor, far gone in their cups. They were at the sentimental stage, throwing their arms around one another and telling each other how much they loved each other. Suddenly, one turned to his companion and said, "Ivan, what hurts me now?" Ivan answered, "Peter, how should I know what hurts you?" Whereupon Peter said, "If you do not know what hurts me, how can you say you love me?" This, said the Rabbi, is the truest definition of love.

It is self-evident that the fostering of true understanding will redound to the well-being both of Jews and of Christians. Jews will be the beneficiaries of a healthier climate in which to live and function and raise their children. By overcoming the age-old heritage of prejudice, Christians will be demonstrating that the sins of the past need not remain the burden of the present or survive as the curse of the future.

The advantages that will accrue to Jews and Christians from mutual respect based upon genuine understanding are incalculable. In addition, the Judeo-Christian tradition will be greatly enriched and benefited by the cross-fertilization that will result from a genuine dialogue between the two faiths. For each religion possesses profound insights of the greatest value that are, however, not free from inherent weaknesses. Hence each tradition can serve as a salutary corrective to the other because of its varied content and emphasis.

Whether a man really loves God can be determined by the love he bears toward his fellow man.

Levi Yitzhak of Berdichev

New Questions
for Jews on Campus

Oscar Groner

Jewish-Christian dialogue is not new to the college campus.
It has been going on for years and has been most fruitful
when addressed to the campus situation in which the religious
worker and serious student find themselves, whether they be
Protestant, Catholic or Jewish. All who work in the campus
milieu face the same religious concerns: the depersonalization
and anonymity of the student in the multi-university; the
mechanization of learning; the problems of war and peace,
today specifically Vietnam and the draft; the anxiety and guilt
created by the "new morality" as these relate to sexual behavior and cheating on examinations; and the general anxieties
of living in the nuclear age.

What is new about today's Jewish-Christian dialogue is the
result of Vatican II and the Catholic-Protestant rapprochement
it engendered. These developments have created new issues in
campus dialogue, not the least of which is confusion about the
word "ecumenical" itself. A newly-appointed part-time Hillel
advisor, a layman, recently expressed the dilemma as follows:

> In my initial meeting with the ministerial faculty, I was
> exposed to a discussion on a topic about which I have very
> little knowledge. According to the other ministers, it
> seems that our school and other major universities in this
> country are using the ecumenical approach to religious
> life on campus.

> Whereas in the past the Newman Club, Wesley Founda-
> tion, etc., operated their own individual programs and

cooperated only in such projects as Religious Emphasis Week, they have now given up such individual programming and are approaching all programming on an ecumenical basis.

They were uncertain as to the role Hillel would play in this structure. I informed them that I hadn't heard anything about this from National and, therefore, could not express the official position until I heard from the parent body. I did, however, express a personal opinion that Hillel would maintain its own program, but would remain a part of the religious complex of the campus.

Does ecumenism include the Jewish community? Obviously not. It represents Christendom in search of community— Christian community. It was never intended to create an amorphous Jewish-Christian religious communion or some other common denominator American faith neither Jewish nor Christian. The tendency to give to the word "ecumenical" this much wider usage must be resisted.

Ecumenism on Campus

Christian ecumenism on campus raises a second, more important, issue for the Jewish community. For the first time, the Hillel rabbi on campus may have to stand alone on campus religious issues.

Not too long ago, the religious polity of the campus was splintered among the Jewish, Roman Catholic, and the broad range of Protestant groups. Within the last ten years, ecumenical trends in Protestantism have brought into being united campus Christian ministries, particularly at the newer schools. Still, there remained a clear three-way distinction among Jewish, Protestant and Catholic approaches to the campus. Today there is a new ecumenical spirit in the air moving in the direction of a united Protestant-Catholic ministry to the campus. The Catholic and Protestant national student organizations are already working jointly to establish a unified national approach. This united ministry expresses itself in joint study commissions on Christian liturgy, in joint action on war and peace, and on the implementation of joint concerns in the area of student activist movements.

The Hillel director and the Jewish student are not excluded from this ecumenical endeavor; on the contrary, they are welcomed wholeheartedly and even find it difficult to refuse tactfully. On the student level there is a good deal of "ecumenical" activity: peace vigils, art festivals, film forums, conferences on war and peace, coffee houses, trialogues on religious themes, dramatic and choral programs, and round-table discussions on liturgy.

The new departure for the Christian ecumenical movement is to break out of the religious foundation building and program and to bring the ministry directly to the campus. More is involved here than ecumenicity. It is part of another pattern, namely, the breakdown of interest on the part of the Christian student in the traditional activities of his campus religious denomination. In other words, part of this movement to the campus grows out of a sense of despair. Another part grows out of the Bonhoeffer influence in Christian theology, which today moves the locus of religious concern from the organized church on campus to the world of the campus itself. To paraphrase Harvey Cox, the secular campus is the paradigm of the secular city. The third ingredient is staff. By de-emphasizing denominational identity, the ecumenical movement frees staff to do certain specialized kinds of tasks. All these trends taken together present the picture of what is happening in the campus ministry from the Christian side.

If we look at these patterns from the Jewish perspective, we see something else. Hillel directors are not as discouraged with our campus ministry as many of the Christian groups seem to be. So far as we can ascertain today, Jewish student response to Hillel programs is not radically different from the level of attainment in earlier years. In some respects, the response is even better.

Jewish College Youth

There are discernible trends which indicate that third and fourth generation Jewish college youth are more accessible to Judaism than their parents ever were. Some foundations report good response to study groups and Institutes of Judaism. The large number of Jewish students interested in observing *kashrut* is a phenomenon which did not exist even seven or eight years ago. There is a great outcry of parents—also new —when Rosh Hashanah and Yom Kippur coincide with registration and with new student week.

The issues here may not be religiosity as much as the greater sense of at-homeness and self-assuredness of the Jewish student on the campus, the feeling that he belongs and that campus life must accommodate itself to his religious needs. This generation of Jewish students refuses to give up its Jewishness in order to "pass." If anything, it reflects a different mood: "If you don't like what I am and what I stand for, that's your problem."

The Jewish task has never been to move out to the world to convert it to Judaism. Whatever influence we may have in the world is by being what we are—Jews—nothing more, nothing less. Traditionally, Christianity has moved out into the world and Jews have stayed within.

Jews and Christians may be going through different cyclical patterns. Christendom wants to break through its own institutions and go back into the world. That has always been its mandate. Jews have been out in the world for the last 150 years and many are now moving back into the Jewish world to find out who they are and where they come from.

Residence Hall Programs

The differing Christian and Jewish approaches to the campus are illustrated in the residence hall program. In this program, campus religious workers are stationed in different living units across the campus all throughout the week. They have offices where they can meet students in formal and informal counseling; they take their meals with students; they lead informal discussion groups and sometimes arrange for regular structured programs. Some campus workers spend little time if any at all at the headquarters denomination building.

In this period of Christian ecumenism, the residence hall program is a natural extension of Christian thinking. The Christian worker takes a stance on campus not as a Methodist, a Presbyterian or a Roman Catholic, but as a Christian human being, a Christian presence without any denominational label.

How far this movement has gone even in the Catholic Church can be seen from the following statement of Thomas Phelan, a Catholic priest: "As a university chaplain, I have a ministry to the university seen as the whole collective of persons and structures, and also a pastoral ministry to my own co-religionists, the Roman Catholic community."

For the Jew, however, who does not see his ministry extending to the campus as a whole and who does not consider the concept of a secular campus a minus quality, the residence hall program is not crucial. We are glad to be involved: by going to the dorms we do meet the Jewish student who will not make his way to the religious foundation, and we do have something important to say as Jews about Western civilization and the issues of our day to the campus as a whole.

But if the involvement of the Hillel director in this program is at the expense of weakening his Foundation program, this is too great a price to pay. We believe that teaching Judaism to Jewish students can best be done at the Hillel Foundation itself. The residence hall program does not function as a mission station or a feeder belt to lead the souls and bodies of students from their place of residence to the Hillel Foundation.

New Challenge

A recent survey of views of Hillel directors on the newer trends in campus interreligious activity shows an awareness of the consequences of the ecumenical movement. There is a difference in attitudes toward "ecumenical" activity depending on the nature of the function. According to Rabbi Joseph Levine, "programming in the area of shared value questions was felt to be one of the most valid forms of ecumenical endeavor involving Jewish students."

Hillel directors favor interreligious activities provided that there is a clear understanding that the unique qualities of the Jewish faith position are in no way impinged. Students should not be left with the impression that they all share one common religious faith. Hillel directors are reluctant to engage in interreligious functions which create the impression that there is a cultural and religious sameness or a commonality of religious views in American life.

Interreligious programs are not to be considered a replacement for individual autonomous creative programming on the part of campus religious groups. J. Claude Evans, writing from the Christian perspective on the current student rebellion against the Church, makes the same point when he states that "coffee houses, jazz masses, theological seminars—good as far as they go—are not enough. Renewal in depth will not result from gimmickry."

The ecumenical movement may revivify the Church, but an ecumenical movement whose power Jews cannot resist may spell the end of Jewish uniqueness. The Jewish community has been struggling ever since its emancipation and particularly in the United States in the last 50 years with the problem of how to maintain Judaism in a free and open society. Religious uniformity is an ominous concept. We fear it. Our primary task is to rediscover our Jewish roots. How we do this without running counter to the ecumenical trends sweeping our world may well be our newest challenge.

An Interreligious Dialogue on The Schema

Vatican Council II's

Declaration on the Jewish People

Since the spiritual patrimony common to Christians and Jews is so great, the Council wishes to foster and commend mutual understanding and esteem. This will be the fruit, above all, of Biblical and theological studies and of brotherly dialogues.

True, the Jewish authorities and those who followed their lead pressed for the death of Christ; still, what happened in his passion cannot be charged against all the Jews, without distinction, then alive, nor against the Jews of today. Although the Church is the new People of God, the Jews should not be represented as rejected by God or accursed, as if this followed from the holy Scriptures. All should see to it, then, that in catechetical work and in the preaching of the word of God they teach nothing save what conforms to the truth of the Gospel and the Spirit of Christ.

Furthermore, in her rejection of every persecution against any man, the Church, mindful of the patrimony she shares with the Jews and led not by political reasons but by the Gospel's spiritual love, decries hatred, persecution, manifestations of anti-Semitism, directed against Jews at any time and by anyone.*

The preceding is the most-discussed section of the Schema, dealing with the crucifixion, Jewish responsibility and anti-Semitism.

In the articles that follow, this passage and other sections of the Schema relating to Jews are discussed by Catholic, Jewish and Protestant authorities.

* For complete text and official Catholic commentary, see *The Church and the Jewish People* by Augustin Cardinal Bea (Harper & Row, N. Y., 1966).

Vatican Council II

An Historic View

Martin A. Cohen

Thanks to a burst of interest on the part of impressive numbers of Catholics, the Catholic-Jewish dialogue has become a reality. Segments in both groups oppose and even assail it. But others, long eager for such colloquy, herald it as the overture to a new era of understanding between the two faiths.

This dialogue is an outgrowth of the Second Vatican Council, the twentieth in a series of Ecumenical Councils that began with the conclave at Nicaea in 325, shortly after Catholicism became the official doxy of the Roman Empire. Like all its predecessors, Vatican II was convoked to deal with problems of surpassing magnitude, which if left unattended might eventually debilitate the Church. Nothing short of such problems could have justified the tremendous expenditures of money and time the Councils entailed.

New Problems for Church

The problems of the contemporary Church are the creations of the twentieth century. The phenomenal increase in human knowledge and education in the past sixty years has brought the advanced countries of the world a large and enlightened Catholic laity and a more diversely cultured priesthood. Both advocate greater contemporaneity in the forms of the Church and opportunities for wider participation in the guidance of its destiny.

The Church has also seen rapidly improving communications shrink the earth to a fraction of its former time-space dimensions. Alien systems of thought, including indifferentism, agnosticism, atheism and Communism, have been brought dangerously close to its citadels of faith.

The traditional balance of power is also being challenged. Europe, the Church's traditional base, has been watching the loss of its vaunted centrality. Non-Christians in many formerly dominated areas chafe at the Church's role in European colonialism, while Catholic inhabitants increasingly resent the disproportional power Europeans continue to wield in the Church hierarchy.

Above all, the last sixty-six years have brought the world's social problems into the foreground of man's concern. No longer satisfied with the glowing promise of next-worldly bliss as recompense for unremedied suffering on earth, disadvantaged peoples have been clamoring for their solution. Religious structures, the Church included, have come to realize that failure to confront them adequately will be tantamount to abdicating power and prestige in the areas of morality and ethics.

The example of the Church supports the axiom that no stucture in society is monolithic. In all ages, the Church hierarchy has encompassed numerous sub-groups spanning the spectrum from conservative to liberal positions. Each sub-group has reacted to the problems of the Church by espousing a platform it has hoped to convert into official Church policy. In times of critical problems and potential disruption of Church leadership, councils have been called to level differences with the hammer of compromise. In the gravest cases the convocations have assumed the scope and appelation of Ecumenical Councils.

Realism of Schema

The purpose of Vatican II is to address itself to the realities of the changing world and to effect an *aggiornamento*, or updating, that will reinvigorate the Church. Its new forms and concepts represent compromises attained through long deliberations. These compromises serve primarily and fundamentally the interests of the Church.

Like documents from other organizations, however liberal, other-directed and altruistic they may be, the schemas emanating from Vatican II must be understood as motivated by self-interest. In the case of the Schema dealing with the Jews, the question to be asked is how it serves the needs of the contemporary Church.

Some Jews, believing the Church to have the same needs and outlook as it did in the nadir of the Middle Ages, insist that the Schema's intent is conversionist. This view, however, overlooks the fact that greater opportunities for conversion than ever before are now open to the Church among more numerous groups. Furthermore, it neglects to consider the Church's prior need to resolve the major problems now facing it and the strong possibility that the Schema dealing with the Jews is somehow related to attempts at their solution. An alternative explanation for the role of the Schema is therefore to be sought.

Indeed, the Church may well see a dual role for the Jews. To begin with, by participating in the dialogue, Jews can testify to the new character of the Church. In a sense, they are put into the position of endorsing Catholic action with which discussion reveals them to be in accord. In this area, Jews, though small in number, can be of inestimable help. Highly educated, socially minded, active in communications and other creative areas, Jews represent an important potential source of support that can hardly be sloughed off in the modern world.

The image of the Jew can serve as a symbol of the Church's new attitude toward non-Catholic peoples. In the Schema on its relations with non-Catholic religions the Church acknowledges the right of religious dissent and denounces all "discrimination against men or harrassment of them because of their race, color, condition in life or religion."

This statement, some claim, was motivated by the Church's concern for Catholic minorities in various lands. Yet the fact remains that such a statement was never previously made, though Catholic minorities often suffered grievously.

To lend credibility to its new posture the Church has found itself compelled to renounce the embarrassing history of Catholic anti-Semitism. It therefore has had to make adjustments in the ideology where this anti-Semitism is rooted. Hence the Schema, a compromise document in which the Church's liberal elements showed up weaker than Jews had hoped.

Jewish Reaction

From a theological view, the Schema is utterly unacceptable to Jews. No Jew can acquiesce in its underlying assumption of the Church's divine calling as spokesman and judge of truth. Nor can any Jew agree with its belief, explicity stated in the document, that its faithful are the "new people of God," replacing the Jews. Besides, Jews deny that the Jewish authorities of the time, let alone other Jews then or later, are in need of exoneration for the death of Jesus.

Nevertheless, from a practical standpoint, the Schema cannot be rejected. Through the layers of theological presuppositions unacceptable to Jews shines the Church's throbbing need to do something about Catholic anti-Semitism for the sake of its new persona. Hence the Church's desire, unmistakably sincere, to draw nearer to the Jews by rectifying old wrongs and creating permanent bridges of communication and understanding.

The dialogue which serves the Church in areas related to the Jews also gives Jews an opportunity to work for a solution of their own problems which may be related to the Church. Foremost among these, of course, is the millennial curse of Catholic anti-Semitism, which continues to this day among large numbers of Catholics everywhere, including the United States.

Historic Jewish-Catholic Relations

The history of the Jewish-Catholic relationship extends over two millennia (for one must go back to the origins of the Church), several continents and a wide variety of politics and cultures. Yet disinterested analysis reveals an indissoluble link between the persecution of Jews and texts sacred to the Church. Statements prejudicial to the Jews in the Gospels and Church Fathers form the foundation for the entire corpus of subsequent anti-Jewish writing and belief. These texts have inspired the conception of the Jews as abased and inferior beings, abandoned by God for their rejection of Jesus and responsible as a group for his death. Also rooted in them are a host of medieval superstitions and libels, ranging from the belief that Jews exuded a peculiar odor to the more serious charges of well poisoning, host desecration and ritual murder.

Nor would it be difficult to demonstrate that this ideology served as the rationale for the manifold expressions of anti-Jewishness in Catholic lands. First is the pervasive and unabating hatred of the mob in every Catholic land where Jews have lived. For the most part, however, the mob's passions could be controlled by the leadership class.

Second, humiliating and often crippling legislation was heaped upon the Jews by Church and non-Church structures alike. These included special taxes, distinctive dress, restrictions of domicile, and even the contemptuous slapping of the face of the leader of the Jewish community by a local Christian leader on Good Friday.

In addition, there were countless outbreaks of mob violence against the Jews, generally at the will and under the captaincy of members of the leadership classes. The persecutors disturbed Jewish stability, confiscated Jewish property, destroyed

Jewish lives and often crowned their activity by expelling the battered remnant of the Jewish community from the afflicted region.

The texts of Catholic anti-Semitism pinnacled by the Gospels and systematized in its theology remain, and their wording can no more be altered than that of the Hebrew Bible or the Talmud. What hope does this leave for the eradication of Catholic anti-Semitism?

Persistence of Anti-Semitism

None, if we are to draw inferences from the statements of some Catholic theologians participating in the dialogue. For instead of coping with the problem in the present and its possible danger in the future, they spend themselves in attempts to sunder Catholic ideology from implication in the persecutions of the past.

Some point out that violence against the Jew has nearly always been linked to economic, social and political upheavals. Hence these causes and not Catholic thought must bear the blame.

Others explain that Catholic doctrine, founded on love, cannot sow persecution, but rather deprecates and condemns all hatred. By implication, persecutors of the Jews, bishops and popes not excluded, strayed from Catholic doctrine. Blame for the persecutions therefore lies squarely on the shoulders of these sinners and not in the domain of Catholic thought.

While the premises of these arguments are correct, their conclusions are defenseless. The role of social unrest is unquestionably fundamental for an understanding of violence: yet there is no a priori reason why the Jews must be its victims. The fact would seem to remain that in every single case Catholic thought provided the ideological base or medium for victimization. And while the persecutors of the Jews may have flouted essential Catholic theology, how many were ever reprimanded for so doing? Some found that their anti-Jewish activities enhanced their reputation for Christian devotion.

And there are still theologians, innocent of the psychology of the persecutor, who follow the ideologists of the Catholic past in projecting the blame for persecutions upon the Jews themselves. Fortunately such thinkers today, though not inconspicuous, are few in number. Most Catholic leaders are aware that, in every Catholic land, Jews lived and worked at the pleasure of their hosts; social and economic activities, even moneylending, were determined by the nation's non-Jewish leadership and subjected to its control.

Such theological analyses, even assuming they are right, do absolutely nothing about the practical problem of Catholic anti-Semitism today.

A Hopeful Note

Yet a study of history provides a ray of hope. It shows that despite countless persecutions, the history of Jews in Catholic lands was not one of unremitting sorrow. Belief in the relentlessness and ubiquity of Jewish suffering stems from a juxtaposition of instances taken from different places. Within the separate regions where Jews lived, a different picture of their history can be limned.

In most areas the Jewish community enjoyed years of stability and security which often surpassed the years of its sorrow. Generally Jewish well-being corresponded to the time of a society's growth and development. Throughout Europe, from the Franco-German center in Gershom's and Rashi's time to Christian Spain and Catholic Poland, Jews were able to amass wealth, attain leisure and unhurriedly add superstructures to their culture. Needless to say, Jews could not have entered any of these territories had the doors been closed, or remained very long if unprotected, or attained prosperity if incessantly victimized by crippling laws and persecution.

In point of fact, Jews were regularly welcomed into these lands. They were treated with dignity and even granted privileges. And they were protected against the rumblings of the mob by none other than the society's most powerful leaders, ecclesiastics as well as laymen, all noble and devout upholders of the Church.

In the labyrinthine history of Jewish-Catholic relations, worthy of fresh and detailed scholarly consideration, we find alongside of instances of nobles persecuting the Jews, examples of others defending them. We find some bishops and kings enacting or enforcing noxious laws against the Jews and others defying episcopal and papal edicts detrimental to them. While some popes were silent in the face of Jewish suffering in Catholic lands, others roundly denounced actions and beliefs prejudicial to the Jews. And regularly, where Jews were expelled from one area—on the grounds of religious ideology—they were welcomed by Catholic leaders in another. The most striking example of this came at the height of the Inquisition in the Iberian Peninsula. At that time Catholic families of Jewish descent, many converted against their will and therefore unreceptive to Catholicism, were being hounded as heretics. Many of those who succeeded in escaping from Spain and Portugal found a haven of refuge in the Papal States.

Of course, the protection extended by Catholic leaders to the Jews was not without its reward. Jews helped to build the economic life of every Catholic land to which they came. They served as disseminators of culture, diplomatic advisers and even as physicians in ordinary to bishops and popes. And they played a vital role in the establishment of political stability.

If one explains the favor shown Jews by Catholic leadership as motivated by self-interest rather than emotion, then it would be only fair to explain their role in the persecution of the Jews on the same basis. Indeed, it is easy to demonstrate that in troubled times the anti-Jewish ideology served well-defined political ends. By arousing the restive masses against the defenseless Jews leadership groups could neutralize revolutionary bids of subordinates and siphon off the discontent of the mob.

Conversely, if Catholic hatred of the Jews is to be considered a motive force in their tragedies, then Catholic respect and indeed affection for the Jew must be included as an element in their eras of achievement. Any belief in the universal hatred of Jews by Catholic leaders is in need of reconsideration.

Thus, though Catholic ideology was always available, it served as a major factor in anti-Semitic violence only when the leadership classes wished it to do so. At all times considerations of need guided its use. When useful, the leadership could effectively neutralize any pejorative interpretations of Catholicism's sacred texts, and, by manifest example, demonstrate toward the Jews the noble and humanitarian ideals which these texts enshrine.

There is every reason to believe that the Catholic groups interested in the current dialogue wish to stress these ideals, and to minimize and effectively neutralize its anti-Jewish texts.

⧼✺⧽

The Creation of Adam

When at last the assent of the angels to the creation of man was given, God said to Gabriel: "Go and fetch Me dust from the four corners of the earth, and I will create man therewith." . . . the dust was taken from all four corners of the earth, so that if a man from the east should happen to die in the west, or a man from the west in the east, the earth should not dare refuse to receive the dead, and tell him to go whence he was taken. Wherever a man chances to die, and wheresoever he is buried, there will he return to the earth from which he sprang.

Legends of the Bible by Louis Ginzberg
(Simon and Schuster, 1956)

Vatican Council II

A Catholic View

Walter M. Abbott, S.J.

The supreme authority of the Catholic Church—Pope and bishops assembled in an Ecumenical Council—has spoken authoritatively about the relationship of Catholics to the Jewish people in the Vatican II pronouncement on the Jews. One of the Council's directives is that Catholics should engage in a dialogue with Jews.

In that dialogue, Catholics will learn that the Jewish people lament the fact that the Council statement contains no profession of contrition, no penitential admission of guilt, no cry of sorrow for the sufferings Christians have inflicted upon Jews over the past sixteen hundred years. Sometimes honored, but more often bruised and battered by history, Jews can never forget. They wonder why their Christian neighbors know little or nothing of those sufferings; they may even suspect that their Christian neighbors know but do not care.

But the truth is that most Christians do not know the terrible history of Christian-Jewish relations. It will take time for them to learn what the problem is.

Vatican Council Statement

The Second Vatican Council's statement on the Jews helps meet this problem. It begins on a positive note by going to the root of what Christianity and Judaism have in common—fatherhood in Abraham:

> As this sacred Synod searches into the mystery of the Church, it recalls the spiritual bond linking the people of the New Covenant with Abraham's stock. For the

Church of Christ acknowledges that, according to the mystery of God's saving design, the beginnings of her faith and her election are already found among the patriarchs, Moses, and the prophets. She professes that all who believe in Christ, Abraham's sons according to faith, are included in the same patriarch's call.

Here the Council Fathers set forth facts that have been neglected, obscured, misinterpreted or denied by some Christians. They insist that the beginnings of the Christian faith are to be found among the patriarchs, Moses and the prophets. The Church proclaims her unity with the "chosen people" of the Old Testament.

The Council Fathers here begin to touch on the history of tension between Christianity and Judaism. There is, first, a reference to the opposition some Jews showed to Christianity —a fact of history that partly explains the subsequent tension. More important, however, is what follows, which presents the Church's official attitude toward the Jews.

Nevertheless, according to the Apostle, the Jews still remain most dear to God because of their Fathers, for He does not repent of the gifts He makes nor of the calls He issues. In company with the prophets and the same Apostle, the Church awaits that day, known to God alone, on which all peoples will address the Lord in a single voice and "serve Him with one accord."

It is important for Catholics to understand that these two sentences are a summary of Biblical understandings.

On Conversion

A reference to the idea of converting the Jews was removed from an earlier version because many Council Fathers thought this inappropriate in a document whose purpose was to establish common goals and interests. The document continues:

Since the spiritual patrimony common to Christians and Jews is thus so great, this sacred Synod wishes to foster and recommend that mutual understanding and respect which is the fruit above all of Biblical and theological studies, and of brotherly dialogues.

The word "mutual" indicates that the Council Fathers hope for two-way communication. Here the Church takes the initiative: we should share Biblical and theological studies, and engage in brotherly dialogue. The Council's earlier Decree on Ecumenism urged Catholics to take the initiative in proposals for dialogue with other Christians. Here the Council Fathers encourage similar dialogue with Jews. On October 1, 1965, four weeks before the statement on the Jews was promulgated by Pope Paul and the Council Fathers, it was announced in Rome that the Catholic Bishops of the United States had established a commission to discover ways to further this dialogue.

It is altogether fitting that the American bishops should have been first with such a move. The possibilities for grassroots dialogue in the United States exceed anything found in any other country because of its large percentage of high school and college graduates. With its pool of educated manpower, the Catholic Church in America has a membership most ready for mass participation in the ecumenical movement. We are in the best position to show the world how the Decree on Ecumenism and the Council's statement on the Jews should be implemented.

On the Deicide

In the Vatican Council's statement on the Jews the Council Fathers identify one of the roots of anti-Semitism: "True, authorities of the Jews and those who followed their lead pressed for the death of Christ." The Gospels recount involvement of Jewish leaders in the arrest and death of Jesus, which has, in fact, been a basic element in the thesis that the Jewish people were therefore guilty of the death of Jesus— a thesis held by some Christians from early times to the present. The Council Fathers repudiate the thesis and its consequences: "Still, what happened in His passion cannot be blamed upon all the Jews then living, without distinction, nor upon the Jews of today." The root has now been pulled up; those who feed upon it feed upon a dead thing.

The Council Fathers proceed to pull up another root of anti-Semitism. Fathers of the Church, notably some Greek Fathers, e.g., St. John Chrysostom and various preachers in the history of the Church, attempted to base a pejorative attitude toward Jews on sacred Scripture. The Second Vatican Council rejects and repudiates this idea:

> Although the Church is the new people of God, the Jews should not be presented as repudiated or cursed by God as if such views followed from the holy Scriptures. All should take pains, then, lest in catechetical instruction

and in the preaching of God's word they teach anything
out of harmony with the truth of the gospel and the spirit
of Christ.

The spirit of Christ is one of love, not hate.

The Council Fathers have been accused by some (who
should know better) of "playing God" and "absolving,"
"forgiving" or "exonerating" the Jews of guilt for the crucifixion of Jesus. These terms were used in newspaper head-
lines describing this section of the Council document. The
Council is, in fact, instructing Catholics to repudiate the
notion of a collective Jewish guilt and to eliminate false views
that in the past have caused Jews to be victims of discrimination. It does not absolve Jews from guilt for the crucifixion:
it knows full well that the Jews were not guilty, and that
the matter of forgiveness for those who were involved was
capably handled by Jesus himself when he said: "Father, forgiven them, for they know not what they do."

As a result of this statement by the Second Vatican Council, no Catholic may quote the Bible to justify calling the
Jews a cursed people or a people repudiated by God. What,
then, of a certain school of interpretation that traces its
lineage back to St. John Chrysostom, and even beyond? We
Catholics repudiate and reject it. Where any of it remains in
our books we must change it.

We have excellent guidelines from Cardinal Bea, the Biblical scholar who was providentially chosen by Pope John to
direct the Catholic Church's work for Christian unity and for
better Christian-Jewish relations. No Catholic can any longer
have any doubt that the verse "His blood be upon us and upon
our children" (Matthew 27:25) is to be understood as the cry
of a Jerusalem mob that has no right to speak for the whole
Jewish people. Christ's own severe words of judgment on
Jerusalem (Matthew 23:37 ff., etc.) do not suggest collective
culpability of the Jewish people for the crucifixion. Rather
they cap a long history of Jerusalem's disobedience to God and
crimes against the prophets, and are to be understood as a
"type" of the universal, final judgment.

On Teaching of Contempt

Whatever passage of the New Testament has been used to
justify the teaching of contempt may be so used no longer.
For example, one passage which has caused much trouble, on
cursory reading, seems to contradict St. Paul's otherwise unan-
imously amiable theology about the Jews:

> . . . the Jews, who killed both the Lord Jesus and the
> prophets, and drove us out, and displease God and oppose
> all men by hindering us from speaking to the Gentiles
> that they may be saved—so as always to fill up the meas-
> ure of their sins. But God's wrath has come upon them
> at last! (I Thess. 2:14-16)

There, it would seem at first glance, as given by hard-
breathing and zealous exegetes of the far right, is the accusa-
tion of deicide (*killed* the *Lord*); there is God's curse upon
them (the *Jews* . . . God's *wrath* has come upon them at last);
there, too, is the world conspiracy that Jews have so cleverly
and diabolically directed throughout history, causing all the
disasters and all the Church's woe (*oppose all men*)—ah, yes,
they are reprobates, repudiated by God (*always . . . fill up* the
measure of their *sins*). Now that the Second Vatican Council
has authoritatively spoken, however ("not . . . repudiated or
cursed by God . . . from the holy Scriptures"), this entire exegesis goes up in smoke.

What, then, does the passage mean? With help from the
Council's Dogmatic Constitution on Divine Revelation, with its
teaching about the proper understanding of the Bible, one can
safely say that this passage, so unlike Paul's usual teaching on
the Jews, is the passionate outburst of an angry and frustrated
bishop who finds that synagogue presidents will not let him
speak, in town after town, but have him locked up for disturbing the peace. Yes, there seems to have been a conspiracy;
each synagogue president sent word ahead warning that a
troublemaker was on the way; this is reminiscent of notices
in the twentieth century Catholic press warning the faithful
about apostate priests coming around.

Old traditions die hard, even after they are exposed as false,
invalid, pernicious. On February 8, 1965, for example, a conference of Coptic Orthodox leaders was convoked in Cairo by
Patriarch Kyrillos VI of Alexandria and attended by delegates
from Ethiopia, Sudan, Jordan and the United Arab Republic.
A resolution was passed "to follow the Bible, which condemns
Jews for Christ's crucifixion, and to regard all resolutions contrary to the text of the Bible as invalid." Nothing that the
Second Vatican Council declared has changed the minds of
those men.

Fortunately, however, most Catholics still believe that the
Pope and the bishops, successors of the apostles, are the
authentic interpreters of sacred Scripture. Before this Council,
only twenty-five verses of the Bible had the distinction of this
kind of authoritative interpretation; to these are now added

the statement of an Ecumenical Council that applies to all Biblical passages about the Jews.

Pope Paul has demonstrated that he is serious about implementing the decrees of Vatican II. The very day the statement on the Jews was promulgated he had his Congregation of Rites and the Archbishop of Trent announce the abolition of the anti-Semitic cult of St. Simon of Trent.

We Catholics must persevere in this spirit; we still have a great deal to prove to the Jews. We cannot rest with one symbolic act. Just as that one act in Italy reverberated around the world—more resonantly than many Christians realize—so too will similar acts build confidence.

If we are honest about the Council's statement on the Jews, we shall have to admit a great many things. We shall have to admit, for example, that St. John Chrysostom's tirades against the Jews are not only contrary to the authentic understanding of holy Scripture; they are also scurrilous. On two counts, therefore—false interpretation of the Bible and violation of the supreme law of charity—the cause of John Chrysostom for canonization would today run into serious difficulties.

Honesty would also compel us to admit that the laws against the Jews passed by the Fourth Lateran Council in 1215 were flagrant violations of the supreme law of charity, and were therefore actually null and void, as subsequent popes in fact regarded them. In Catholic Church histories, the Fourth Lateran Council is presented as the greatest Council of the Middle Ages because it did such magnificent work on Catholic doctrine about sacraments. Little or nothing is said in our seminary courses about the laws against the Jews. As a result, most priests and most of the laity know nothing about them. Jews remember them, however. In fact, some Jews trace a great deal of the strength of Nazism to those laws.

The Christian may now tell his Jewish friend that if there was anti-Semitism in those laws, it is now repudiated by the Second Vatican Council: "The Church . . . deplores the hatred, persecutions, and displays of anti-Semitism directed against the Jews at any time and from any source."

He can also explain the distinction between disciplinary laws and doctrinal statements. The four laws of the Lateran Council were disciplinary, therefore changeable; they did not assert any teaching of the Church. On the other hand, the statement of Vatican II, which is doctrinal and therefore unchangeable, repudiates and rejects the thinking that lay behind the discriminatory laws of Lateran IV.

Jewish scholars who had hoped that the Second Vatican Council would explicitly repudiate the discriminatory laws of the Fourth Lateran Council can be assured that that repudiation is implicit: ". . . any time and from any source." This may not be a profession of contrition, a penitential admission of guilt, a cry of sorrow for the sufferings that resulted from those laws, but it is nonetheless a remarkable step. If the statement of the Council is implemented by Catholics in their minds and hearts, there will be profession of sorrow where it matters most—in the hearts of men. Pope John and Pope Paul have set the example for all of us. Good deeds like these are worth more than even the words of Councils.

The Catholic Task

When will we have done enough to prove our love for our privileged brethren, the Jews? Never. But there is one great act which many Jews would joyfully accept as sufficient proof that we have taken the Second Vatican Council seriously: the deletion from our liturgy of all passages—many of them readings from Scripture—which might cultivate contempt for Jews.

We are far from having done enough for the reformation of our liturgy. Pope Pius XII and Pope John deleted pejorative references to Jews from a Good Friday prayer, and Pope Paul had the offending prayer extensively revised (now it is entitled "For the Jews," instead of "For the Conversion of the Jews"). These were steps in the right direction of mutual understanding and respect for which the Second Vatican Council calls. But the reading of the Gospel during the Pope's Mass at Yankee Stadium reminded us vividly that better selection has to be made of liturgical readings. Millions of viewers gasped when they heard the seminarian read the opening sentence of the passage with its reference to the disciples "gathered together for fear of the Jews" (John 20:19).

We must give a great deal of thought to this problem. Pope John asked for the attention of the world and got it. The Second Vatican Council three times formally asked for the attention of the world, and got it: in its Opening Message, in its Declaration on Religious Freedom, in its Pastoral Constitution on the Church in the Modern World—each addressed to all mankind. The world is watching the Catholic Church.

It is not a matter of changing the Bible; it is not a matter of deleting passages from the New Testament. Our Jewish brethren will surely understand that it is less possible for us to change the Bible than for them to change the Talmud. It is simply a matter of choosing better passages for public worship. We cannot avoid the problem. We cannot turn away the help and advice of the watching world in this matter.

Vatican Council II

A Jewish View

Arthur Gilbert

Several years ago a group of Jewish scholars undertook a study of "anti-Jewish elements in the Catholic liturgy." As yet unpublished, this survey reviewed prayerbooks used in parish churches and cathedrals and analyzed at least fifty officially approved, recently published commentaries upon the liturgy.

The study revealed many references to Jews of a harsh and inflammatory nature. The liturgy included medieval hymns that speak of "a horde of lying Jews" and of Jews as "a heinous brood." Even more disturbing were Catholic commentaries, of recent date, that charge Jews with guilt for the crucifixion and interpret their suffering as proper punishment.

Some of the selections from the Patristic literature, the only homiletic literature elevated into the integral service of the Church during Holy Week, are of such a nature that a defamatory stereotype of the Jew is reinforced and encouraged. The Gospel lessons of the Triduum taken from St. John refer to "the Jews" as though all Jews in a collective sense are to be considered enemies of Jesus.

Contemporary Bible scholars are quick to point out that the Gospel does not mean to condemn all Jews nor to separate Jesus and his followers from their Jewish kinship. But the selections from the Church Fathers used in the Holy Week services to explain and elaborate the Scriptural readings offer no such reconciling explanations. Instead they contribute to the image of the Jews as a base and villainous people.

St. Augustine is on record as having called upon Christians to treat Jews with a certain benevolence and to recognize their importance to the Church as the living witnesses of Christian claims. The contemporary Jew is uneasy about such a view. But it is not even this passage from Augustine's that is included in the Holy Week prayers. Instead, it is the commentary from St. Augustine on the Psalms that is recited during the Nocturn of Good Friday:

> Let not the Jews say: We did not kill Jesus Christ—for exactly this was in their minds when they handed him over to Pilate, so that they themselves might appear innocent of his death . . . For when Pilate said to them: You kill him—they replied: We are not permitted to kill anyone. They wanted to shift the iniquity of their crime to a human judge, but did they deceive the Divine Judge? Whatever Pilate did he was to a certain extent an accessory, but in comparison with them [the Jews] he was much more innocent . . . Yet he [Pilate] pronounced the verdict and committed him to be crucified and thus kill him. In which way have you [the Jews] killed him? With the sword of the tongue—for you sharpened your tongues. And when did you slay him—when you cried out crucify, crucify!

If one demurs that such a selection from the Church Fathers has to be understood in terms of the tensions and conflicts, the world view and philosophies at that time, how shall we account for the fact that Catholic commentaries on the liturgy written only recently still operate with the view that Jewish history must be interpreted in light of the deicide?

In J. F. Stedman's *My Lenten Missal* (New York, 1956), we find the following reading for Thursday of Passion Week:

> In these modern days the Jews are still dispersed in every nation in a condition worse than exile. They have been atoning these 1900 years for the greatest of all crimes committed when an entire nation rejected, crucified, and shed the Blood of the Son of God.

Or consider the following excerpt from Father Gueranger's commentary *The Liturgical Year* (Newman Press, 1947):

> Jerusalem is doomed to be a slave . . . She drew this frightful curse upon herself by the crimes she committed against the Son of God . . .

The mark of Parricide and Deicide here fastens on this ungrateful and sacrilegious people; Cain-like they shall wander fugitives on the earth. Eighteen hundred years, and more, have passed since then; slavery, misery and contempt have been their portions but the mark is still upon them . . .

Passages like these serve to reinforce the Jewish conviction that it was exactly through such teachings which, throughout the centuries, had become an integral part of Christian prayers, sermons, Bible lessons and commentaries, that an atmosphere was created in which anti-Semitism flourished.

Background of Schema

It was, in fact, to dispel such interpretations as authentic to Christianity that the Vatican Council undertook its effort to issue a declaration on Judaism. And it was because so large a group of conservative theologians believed the traditional interpretations of Jewish collective guilt and punishment to be the proper reading of the Gospel that the Council had to struggle so long to produce its document.

Political pressures on the Council to avoid a declaration on Judaism were not decisive. In accounting for the final amendments to the text, we must consider the Council's more central task: to articulate in an authoritative way how Catholics ought to read and understand those passages in Scripture that speak of the Jews in a harsh and condemnatory fashion.

Many of the Church Fathers and popes, as a matter of Church policy, had stimulated contempt for the Jews and encouraged civil legislation that consigned Jews to a social and cultural status outside the bounds of the civilized community. Jews were made into a pariah people, and they became vulnerable to pogrom and pillage, persecution and prejudice.

There were popes who rescued Jews from the excesses of over-zealous fanatics, for the Church never officially condoned violence directed against Jews, nor did it approve of enforced conversion. Yet the contempt fostered by the Church inevitably made the Jew the victim of fanaticism, violence and mass murder.

Anti-Semitism served a wide variety of secular purposes. Hatred of Jews protected Christians, in the early days of the Church, from possible backsliding or contamination from the influence of the teachings of Judaism. Eventually, Jews became the landless peddlers of second-hand merchandise, the vulnerable source of easy capital, the aliens who were blamed for plague and pestilence, charged with responsibility for liberalism and revolution. The Crusaders tempered their steel on the flesh of helpless Jews. Spain sought a unified society through the expulsion of Jews. The Russian Czars used Jews as justification for repression of all human liberty.

And, finally, Nazis measured their alleged racial superiority against the "inferiority" of a people led to slaughter. Anti-Semitism has always been most pervasive where there is something to be gained—economic, social, political or psychological—from the denigration and persecution of Jews.

Present-Day Religious Anti-Semitism

But for the Jew there remains one bitter truth: anti-Semitism in its more barbaric form has been a disease of Christian-influenced civilization. There is basis for the feeling that Christian teachings are primarily responsible for the fact that Jews throughout history have been singled out in every Western country for scorn and hatred.

As Father Hans Kung has courageously stated: "The monstrous crime of Nazi anti-Semitism would have been impossible without the Christian anti-Semitism of more than 1500 years, an anti-Semitism that was even manifest in the Council debate."

The University of California has recently published, with the support of the Anti-Defamation League, the most exhaustive and authoritative study of the Christian roots of anti-Semitism ever undertaken. Entitled *Christian Beliefs and Anti-Semitism* the Christian authors of this sociological study, Charles Glock and Rodney Stark, demonstrate the shocking correlation between certain religious beliefs and anti-Semitism.

Sixty-one percent of American Catholics believe that the Jews were responsible for crucifying Christ. Seventy-one percent attribute malevolent reasons to account for the Jewish rejection of Jesus. Fourteen percent believe that the Jews can never be forgiven for what they did to Jesus until they accept him as the true savior, and 32 percent are uncertain whether the Jews will ever be forgiven. Eleven percent believe that the reason Jews have so much trouble is because God is punishing them for rejecting Jesus.

The most revealing statistic is that 83 percent of those Catholics who believed that the Jews were most guilty for the crucifixion, or that the Jews were not to be forgiven until they accepted Jesus as the Christ, were the very ones who scored high or medium-high in anti-Semitism. On the other hand, only six percent of those Catholics who rejected those distorted religious interpretations scored high or medium-high in secular anti-Semitism.

Glock and Stark strongly suggest an unmistakable link between the holding of religious views that foster bigotry and the possibility that such a person will succumb, as well, to negative images of the Jew in the secular culture.

Incidentally, only 19 percent of American Catholics think of Peter and Paul and the Apostles as Jews, whereas 47 percent identify Judas as a Jew. The Christianization of the Old Testament has reached such a point that 15 percent of American Catholics identify Moses, David and Solomon as Christians rather than as Jews and 11 percent suggest that the people picked by God in the Old Testament to be His chosen people were Christians.

Some critics of the Glock and Stark study have suggested that the causal explanations should be reversed. It is not that religious teachings foster anti-Semitism; rather Catholics who are anti-Semitic misuse these teachings in order to justify their prejudice, which derives from secular motivations.

Without doubt anti-Semites will use any support they can find, and the hallowed teachings of the Church are a most suitable cloak for malevolence of a secular nature. The Church's responsibility, nevertheless, remains clear. It must both reject such teachings as may be used to support anti-Semitism and condemn anti-Semitism itself. Acknowledging its own contribution to anti-Semitism, the Church must go out of its way to emphasize its origins in Judaism and its appreciation for the contribution that Jews and Judaism still make to the persistence of God's truth among men.

A Five-Fold Program

To achieve a better future for Jewish-Christian relations I suggest the following five-fold program. The Church should:

1. Repudiate those teachings that lend themselves to misuse by anti-Semites.
2. Condemn anti-Semitism wherever it is found in any form.
3. Acknowledge its own part in creating an environment in which anti-Semitism can flourish.
4. Emphasize Christianity's spiritual relationship to Judaism.
5. And, finally, encourage an attitude of respect for the continuing vitality of Judaism.

The Church today recognizes anti-Semitism to be a scandalous social disorder, against which Catholics ought to marshal their fullest resources. As the Constitution on the Church in the Modern World explicitly affirms: "Every type of discrimination . . . is to be overcome and eradicated as contrary to God's intent."

In at least five different ways in the Decree on Non-Christian Religions the Council Fathers assert that the Church "reproves," "decries," "considers reprehensible" any act of discrimination against any man; and anti-Semitism is named explicitly. This is language strong enough to communicate the convictions of the Church. Many Jews would have been even more reassured, however, had this unequivocal attack on anti-Semitism been coupled with an equally forthright acknowledgment by the Church of its own involvement in the history of anti-Semitism.

In the revolutionary Schema on Ecumenism the Catholic Church found it possible to seek the forgiveness of Protestant and Orthodox Christians for any wrongs Catholics may have perpetrated in bringing about the scandal of disunity. No such note of contrition was evoked in the Church's attitude toward Jews. In fact, twice in his presentation of the Schema, Cardinal Bea assured the Council Fathers that he had no intention of assigning to religious teachings a "primary responsibility" for anti-Semitism. Bea underscored the secular motivations for anti-Semitism, suggesting that the primary reason for the Council's consideration of Christian beliefs with regard to Jews, at this point in history, was the need to respond to the damage caused by the propaganda of Nazism. In Jewish estimation this was an equivocation!

Steps Being Taken

Fortunately Jews are not alone in assessing the Council's silence on this issue as a defect. Father Edward Flannery, who now serves on the American Catholic Bishops' Subcommission on Catholic-Jewish Relations, has written: "The Declaration's main defect was a failure to refer contritely to the role the Church played in the development of anti-Semitism throughout Christian history . . . Anti-Semitism despite all denials is still widespread among Catholics and much of it is still attributed to religious reasons." Noting that Catholics tended to repress any knowledge of the sufferings of Jews at the hands of Church leaders, Father Flannery warns that such pages of history "must be reinserted in our histories and published if the Jewish-Catholic dialogue is to advance and survive."

Such a knowledge of past history is a requirement if sentiment opposed to anti-Semitism is to become a reality in deed. Not only will such knowledge provide the wisdom that may restrain Catholics from ever again making the same errors;

but even more importantly, Catholics cannot address the Jew knowledgeably unless they know how history has influenced him.

In America, at least, it is clear that the conciliar declaration will be used as an instrument of penitence and reconciliation. The Benedictine Father, Benedict M. Ashley, speaking at a Jewish-Christian symposium at Rosary College, interpreted the Council's Declaration to be "essentially a confession by Catholics of their own guilt in the persecution of the Jews throughout 2,000 years. But if we Catholics," he added, "are not absolving the Jews we are seeking absolution of our own guilt through honest confession and resolution to work against anti-Semitism and all forms of racial or religious discrimination."

In this country, too, the Bishops' Commission for Ecumenical Affairs has extended itself in order to give reality to such an interpretation. In its recently published recommendations for diocesan commissions for ecumenical affairs the Bishops' Commission acknowledged that "the ecumenical movement in its strictest sense . . . refers to the efforts to promote Christian unity and does not properly apply to the relationships with non-Christian communities."

Nevertheless, it asserts, "the Commission should see a full measure of cooperation with these religious groups, *notably the Jewish communities*. It might be advisable, "it suggests," to designate at least one member, if not more, of the Commission, to give special attention to fostering mutual understanding and cooperation in the light of the local situation." Not everywhere has this directive been followed but at least a beginning has been made.

New Guidelines

More recently, the Bishops' Subcommission on Education for Ecumenism adopted a series of guidelines for Catholic education. These include the following:

> It must be recognized that although a primary concern of ecumenism is understanding and unity among those who share fellowship in Christ, its movement carries us to search for an understanding of and dialogue with all those who recognize our inescapable solidarity, with all who believe in God or indeed only the brotherhood of man.

The Subcommission then called upon Catholic schools to maintain contact with other traditions and their scholars. "Wherever possible," it said, "teachers from these other traditions should present this material. This is especially true at secondary and higher levels of education . . . Ecumenism requires that Catholics become aware of any religious prejudices and negative attitudes they harbor and strive for their elimination."

Catholic publishers are now preparing text books to be used in Catholic high schools and universities to supplement teaching in theology and in history. Jewish scholars have been invited to give courses in Catholic colleges and seminaries. Institutes on Jewish Studies are now under preparation for matriculation by seminarians, college and seminary faculty, librarians, and the faculty of Catholic parochial schools. These are important and significant evidences of the Church's intention to change the tragic past pattern of Jewish-Christian relations. The Catholic Church thus emerges as a leading force in the effort to achieve inter-religious understanding.

The Declaration's most difficult task was a clarification for Catholics of the Church's relation to the Jewish people of old. Another important achievement was its clear interpretation of the Scriptural passages dealing with the Jews, passages that in past generations had been harshly misused even by sainted Church Fathers and the theologians.

The Council acknowledges at several points in various conciliar decrees its spiritual ties with the Jews through that which is Hebraic or Biblical in the Christian faith. Through the Jews, God not only provided the Church with a way of salvation but through that which in the ancient Hebraic tradition still endures He continues His ministry to mankind.

The Hebrew Bible with its sublime teachings about God, wisdom about human life and rich treasury of prayers, the abiding Jewish sense of community, the unextinguished concern of Judaism for social justice, the assurance of God's fidelity by virtue of His unbroken promise to His people of old—these are all tokens of God in the Jewish people.

Thus the Council could declare with conviction: "Jews remain dear to God. Their election is not revoked. Neither the Jews of the past, nor of this day, can be held accountable for the crucifixion. Jews are not an accursed or reprobate people."

Change of Texts

But what about the harsh passages in Christian Scripture? The text of the Declaration does not itself deal with these at length, but in a series of conditional clauses that were introduced into the final text—much to the chagrin of most Jews— the Council Fathers tried to acknowledge what they believed to be true in these assertions and to delimit their consequences.

Despite Jerusalem's blindness, despite the rejection of the

Gospel by most Jews, said the Council, it would be wrong for Christians to deduce that there is a collective guilt for all Jews, a corporate punishment for all Jews, a revocation of God's gifts to the Jews. An anti-Semite, or for that matter a conservative Biblical scholar, may not henceforth use words of Scripture to fasten upon Jews a guilt of "Parricide" or "Deicide" or a justification for Jewish suffering.

In the explanations prepared for the Bishops, Cardinal Bea's Secretariat added additional notes for Bible study that will become crucial in future years. Many of these notes as well as his own Biblical interpretation are included in Cardinal Bea's new book,* in which he attempts to help the Catholic understand exactly how the harsh passages in Scripture are to be understood. He provides historic and exegetical insights that clarify the inability of Jews en masse to accept the Christian claims and shed light on those passages that deal with Jerusalem's fall or the dispersion of the Jewish people.

Such commentaries, one hopes, will replace those now available for priests and laity. It is not too soon to prepare new Lenten Missals that will speak of the Jews in a new language, fashioned by the spirit of ecumenism and in accordance with the directives of the Council.

Unfortunately, the Catholic community has already muffed a most significant occasion. In a fantastically brilliant move Catholics have accepted for their own use a slightly modified version of the Protestant-created RSV Bible. This was indeed an ecumenical achievement of great moment. But the Catholic notes at the end of this volume, so crucial for the Catholic's understanding of the Biblical text, are inadequate if not offensive in reference to Jews. Nowhere is there a clarification of the Biblical texts referring to Jews which evoke anything of the spirit that predominated at the Council. Certainly someone, somehow, within Catholic educational structures must realize that the issue of Jewish-Christian relations is of such importance that an opportunity such as this must never again be missed. .

Finally, there is among Cardinal Bea's explanations one observation sure to disturb Jews. It comes exactly at that point where the Church feels compelled to define herself in relation to others. Cardinal Bea asserts that whereas the Jews in a collective sense were not punished by a revocation of their election "according to the flesh" they did lose their special status as the people of God. From the definition of the people of God given in the Constitution on the Church it would seem that the Jews are, indeed, excluded. Bea explains that the Jews are no longer the people of God, not because this has been

The Church and the Jewish People (Harper & Row, 1966).

completely rejected as a punishment, but simply because "their function of preparing the Kingdom of God terminated with the coming of Jesus and with the foundation of the Church."

Jews and Christians Need Each Other

Jews cannot accept this conclusion, nor do we even understand it in light of other conciliar assertions regarding the Truth of God which has been placed in trust among other religions. We sense a tension between the assertion that the Jew remains God's elect, that His gifts to the Jews are irrevocable, that there is among them a ray of truth, that they have a continuing and abiding message for mankind, and the presumption that Jews are no longer among the people of God, no longer a sign in man's quest for salvation.

It is our strong conviction that we do confront the living God within the structures of the Jewish community. But there is little point in countering Christian triumphalism with an assertion of Jewish pride. In addition to sharing the gifts of God, Jews and Christians also share in humanity. That means that both of us are prone to error. Neither of us is so wise that we can at once encompass all of God's truth. This means that we share together in the anguish of our inadequacies and in the experience of insensitivity in the face of gigantic problems of human suffering, hatred and war. It means that we need each other.

Christians call themselves the people of God and Jews consider themselves to be God's Israel. God's spirit must be hovering over both of us. He will want to use us in His service, and He calls on us to be a blessing to men and a light to nations.

We hold that all religions have a common aim, toward which they tend in different ways. Each employs parables and images, according to the style of its generation and country, and suitable to the intelligence of its followers, but all aim to lead people to justice, truth and bliss.

Levi ben Abraham

Vatican Council II

A Protestant View

Reinhold Niebuhr

Our nation has been ethnically and religiously pluralistic from its birth. This diversity was substantially increased by the immigrations of the nineteenth century, which brought men of all races and of two religions, Roman Catholicism and Judaism. They challenged the dominant Protestant, Anglo-Saxon group. The nation was troubled by these minority groups and the resulting ferment of racial and religious rivalries and prejudices.

The immigration of the nineteenth century established the largest Jewish community in any Western democratic nation. Both its size and its native talents—which an expanding system of higher education in an affluent nation soon gave valued opportunities in all the arts and sciences—made for an eminence of Jews in all the realms of culture: business, law, politics, journalism and the theatre. Their intellectual talents gave our American culture a quality unique among Western nations.

Jewish-Christian Differences

The Jews were subject to the hazard of a double divergence from the majoritarian Christians. Ethnically, they were obviously not as ready to be melted down in our famed melting pot. A people who until recently lacked a homeland, they had survived the millennia of their Diaspora in all nations. They had persisted in expressing their collective survival impulse—usually by insisting on endogamous marriages and

*Reprinted from *Christianity and Crisis*, December 12, 1966; copyright 1966 by *Christianity and Crisis, Inc.*

strict religious observances, chiefly with regard to the Sabbath and dietary laws—to mark their unique racial identity.

Their theological divergence from the surrounding Christian faith was even more pronounced than their rigorous observance of traditional ritual. They did not accept as their Messiah the Christ of the New Testament, whom ages of Christian piety had identified not only as the expected Messiah of Hebraic prophetic hopes but also the Savior of mankind.

The differences between Jew and Christian on this issue were eloquently defined by the late Martin Buber. Speaking to an audience of Dutch clergymen, he explained: "To the Christian, the Jew is a stubborn fellow who in an unredeemed world is still waiting for the Messiah. To the Jew, world affirms that redemption has somehow or other taken place."

Many Christians might affirm a more exact definition of their faith to be: "To the Jews, the Christian is a heedless fellow who in an unredeemed world affirms that redemption has been initiated." But Buber's definition would certainly be accurate in describing many conventional Christian claims about Christ, for these too often apply christological categories to the Prophets of Israel that not only violate their historical significance but rob their message of historical and social relevance.

The differences of the two faiths concerning the position of Christ were heightened when early Christianity sought to translate the Messianic terms of Hebrew religious hope into the categories of Greek metaphysics. It would be fruitless here to recount the many heresies eliminated before the doctrine of Christ's "two natures" and the theology of Nicaea were defined, establishing the framework of Christian orthodoxy.

Needless to say, this orthodoxy was felt by the Jewish community as an affront to its rigorous monotheism. For Jews to regard a full-blown Christian orthodoxy as anything but a Hellenistic corruption of their Hebraic faith was impossible. It has proved equally difficult for them to realize that many modern Christians, who find metaphysical definitions of the nature and mission of Christ embarrassing, nevertheless persist in cultivating a Christ-centered piety. For many Christians attribute to the person and teachings of Christ, and to the symbolic significance of the whole drama of his life and death on the cross, the secret of the universal appeal to Christianity. To them, Christianity as "the new Israel of God" contains the historical revelation granted to the Chosen People as well as the "light to lighten the Gentiles."

In short, the chasm between the two faiths, which modern
tolerance must now bridge, is formidable. The reasons why
the Jews would not accept the Christian definition of the
place of Christ in any scheme of salvation were many. There
were also many reasons why the Christian majority in this
and in other nations has used religious prejudice to justify
its racial animosity against the Jewish minority. The historic fact of the rejection of Christ was singled out by Christians as a mark of Jewish moral perversity.

Our Common Ground

This past history lays upon Christians today the burdens
of eliminating the religious dimensions of anti-Semitism.
They must, despite all dogmatic difficulties arising from
their own presuppositions, recognize the Jewish faith to be
authentically autonomous.

This means that American Protestants should remove Jews
from the scope of Christian missionary activity; that is, they
should cease to support traditional "missions to the Jews."
This step does not exclude individual conversions from one
faith to another, whether prompted by marriage or special
personal needs. But any conversion prompted by christological
debates obscures the common spiritual and moral factors
in both religions, which are usually a Christian inheritance
from the older Jewish faith.

One must note, for example, the devotional literature of
the Hebrew Scriptures—particularly the Prophets and the
Psalms—that Christians, especially those in the liturgical
traditions, avail themselves of in their worship, corporate
and solitary. A second element is the radical ethic of social
justice of the Prophets of Israel, though Jews might not
regard this as common. They would be inclined to emphasize
an ethic of social justice that distinguishes Hebraic moral
norms from too individualistic, particularly Protestant, moral
norms.

Liberal Protestants of the Social Gospel tradition, however,
would regard the teachings of the Prophets as common and
authoritative. For them, the radical demands of justice, as
expressed in Amos and Isaiah, are a corrective for the irrelevant individualism and perfectionism of Protestantism. En-
shrined in the sacred Scriptures of both Judaism and of Christianity, they provide ultimate norms for man's collective
relations.

The final important element is inherited from Hebraic
spirituality. Both Jews and Christians have sought to give

meaning to man's existence, which is the primary function of all religious faith, by incorporating the vast panorama of the human drama into their universe of meaning. Because history is so full of patches of meaninglessness, so full of the cross-purposes of nature and human ambitions, the effort to give meaning to man's life has been hazardous. Men have the perilous freedom of becoming agents of history even while they remain creatures of nature.

Both Christianity and Judaism have, therefore, produced Messianic expectations in their efforts to find a resolution of the problems of history. These hopes were the measure of their rejection of the undifferentiated eternity of mystic faiths. Mysticism is the mark of man's flight from history and its confusions, and thus may be defined as the nemesis of man's quest for the meaning of existence. It affirms meaning by denying meaning to man's historic existence, including the reality of Kierkegaard's "existing individual."

The inevitable concomitant of a faith that is related to history is the prophetic vision of a Messianic age in which a transfigured history is guaranteed by a transformed nature, as in Isaiah's classic text: ". . . the leopard shall lie down with the kid . . . and a little child shall lead them" (Isaiah 11:6). Though the Messianic images are preposterous, they are not as dangerous as Stalin's utopian heaven on earth, nor as irrelevant as the mystical heaven of Plotinus, which annuls, rather than transmutes, all historical realities.

"All Semites" and Anti-Semitism

The common interest in and emphasis upon our historic responsibilities is the chief heritage of the Jewish faith bequeathed to Christendom. It is responsible for the historical dynamism of Western culture. This bequest makes it particularly important that Christians express their gratitude to the older faith by removing all causes of enmity between them as distinct—but also very intimately related—faiths. In the Nazi era, Pope Pius XII expressed the affinity between the two faiths in the words: "Spiritually we are all Semites."

This reconciliation presents some very difficult problems for the Christian majority. One is that the New Testament, specifically its record of Christ's life in the Gospels, is obviously influenced by Christian ideological viewpoints prompted by the contest between the synagogue and the early church. Thus, the Gospel records show the persistent and perverse failure of many of Jesus' contemporaries to recognize that he was, in fact, the Messiah. It is important that as many

Christian laymen as possible understand this early conflict between church and synagogue, which the historians and scholars of both faiths have described with only minor disagreement.

The frankly anti-Semitic tone of the Gospel of St. John presents a special problem. It consistently describes the enemies of Christ as "the Jews," thereby obscuring the Jewish character of all of his disciples. Jews are quite right in suggesting that the Johannine gospel is a pregnant source of anti-Semitism, at least for the unlearned. Anyone who has attended the famous Oberammergau Passion Play, whose narrative is taken from the Fourth Gospel, would have no doubt about this.

The Schema Challenges Protestants

Protestants may well be challenged by the fact that Vatican II undertook to allay much religiously inspired anti-Semitism by its pronouncement on the relations of Christians to Jews. Also, they may be instructed about the tortuous history of this pronouncement and the virtues and weaknesses of the final version. Cardinal Bea, the late Pope John XXIII's alter ego, took the precaution of inviting friendly Jewish theologians as observers. Their reaction to the unsatisfactory first draft prompted a revision they accepted with some satisfaction.

A final estimate of the Council's pronouncement on the relations between Christians and Jews must be made, however, not by Protestant minds but through the double vision with which a partly secular and partly religious culture fortunately has endowed many modern minds. We must all appreciate the fact that a Catholic council has taken measures to allay the religious prejudices that are perhaps the chief source of the animus against Jews.

Modern minds endowed with this double vision, derived from both Protestant and historical insights, will appreciate the achievement of the Council in implicitly recognizing the authentic autonomy of the Jewish faith by the simple expedient of ignoring the Pauline cry of anguish: ". . . my heart's desire . . . for them [Israel] is that they might be saved" (Rom. 10:1). The Pauline hope for the conversion of the Jews had been the root of a Christian disposition, more authoritative among scripturally-minded Protestants than among Catholics, to regard tolerance of Judaism as merely preliminary to its final absorption in the Christian faith. Naturally this was offensive to the Jews' age-old consciousness of their religious identity.

In addition, the Vatican Council pronouncement absolved the Jews of guilt in the crucifixion of Christ and warned against the moral evils of anti-Semitic hatred. The chief questions about these two propositions have to do with the tardiness of their important and healing insights. One might well wonder why centuries passed before the Church repudiated the most vulgar of anti-Semitic epithets: "Christ-killers." This repudiation of the Jews' responsibility for Christ's crucifixion quite understandably emphasized the symbolic significance of his atoning death in the context of the faith of the early church. Raised to symbolic proportions, the Cross makes all men guilty of the death of the Savior.

Our generation is more aware of the nature and sources of group prejudices and must find the statement of the Vatican Council about the Jews relatively satisfactory. Its condemnation of anti-Semitism and its plea for universal respect for all men are drawn from the universalism of Stoicism, the Hebrew Prophets and Christianity. Albeit belatedly, Vatican II did acknowledge that bigotry, derived from a dogmatic interpretation of history, is inconsistent with the authentic universalism that should inform all high religions of whatever particular dogmatic content.

This brave break with previous Christian attitudes was informed by a genuine Christian universalism. One might add that this universalism was "Christian" in the sense that Jesus' own teachings contained the warning: "For if you love them that love you, what reward have you?" (Matt. 5:46)

But one must also acknowledge that both Paul and Augustine drew upon Stoic universalism in the rigor of their demand for a universal Christian community. The Pauline universalism was clearly meant to assure the universality of the Church, which was "the Body of Christ." So Paul wrote idealistically: "In Christ there is neither Jew nor Greek, neither bond nor free" (Gal. 3:28).

But one is left embarrassed by the statement of this idealism without admitting the involvement of the Christian Church through the ages in persecution of the Jews precisely because an inclusive religious community will not protect any dissident who, for reasons of faith, does not choose to be included in the community. Must not any Christian pronouncement inspired by Pauline universalism express at least an awareness of the fact that through the long medieval period, this universalism did not protect Jews from persecution when they did not avail themselves of the security of Christian faith?

We have been critical of Vatican II's pronouncement about the relations of Christians to Jews from a "modern" perspective rather than a purely Protestant one. On one point, however, the churches of the Reformation are clearly less free than the Roman Catholic Church.

The strength of Biblical authority in these churches has given the Pauline expression of anguished hope in Romans 10 so much prestige that no Protestant ecumenical assembly has ever dared question the legitimacy of Christian missions to the Jews, though these missions have negated every gesture of recognition of our common Biblical inheritance. When some of us questioned the ecumenical wisdom of these not too successful missions to the Jews, we were met with sympathy as well as a warning that our concern was "heretical."

What Christians Must Do

My late brother, Prof. H. Richard Niebuhr, of the Yale Divinity School, was, I think, the first Protestant theologian to affirm unequivocally that the religious affinities of Jew and Christian were so great that Christians must leave the Jews to solve their moral and religious problems without any help from these missions. His judgment did not bear any official fruit, and the witness of many of us was also of no effect for reasons we have reviewed.

I am glad to report that it was the witness of a Christian layman, Charles Taft, a distinguished Episcopal representative to the World Council of Churches (WCC), that gave the most eloquent evidence of both an ecumenical spirit toward the Jews on the part of Protestant Christians and also a striking example of how the inspired common sense of an open society could support and aid this spirit.

When the usual question about these missions came up on the agenda of the Evanston Assembly of the WCC in 1954. Mr. Taft simply recorded his dissent from this traditional project. He said he would not think of trying to convert his distinguished Jewish friend and partner to his own faith. He was persuasive enough to allay the uneasiness about our failure to solve the unsolved religious problem between Christians and Jews.

As American Christians we should be concerned about this remaining religious root of racial hatred. But we may also take some satisfaction that the beneficent impulses of an open society, plus the distinction of the Jews in all our cultural, business and political life, have refuted the most odious racial libels against them.

We must recognize the evil of the anachronistic pockets of anti-Semitism that remain in the exclusion of Jews from our clubs, fraternities, suburban residential areas and employment opportunities. They are too absurd to have a long life in our pluralistic democracy. Our achievements, without a resolution of the religious problems between us, may be threatened by antagonisms, inherited by our children through the bigotry transmitted in our religious educational programs. Fortunately a commission of Catholics, Protestants and Jews is working even now to erase these sources of religious bigotry from the texts used in our Sunday schools.

It is impossible to close this survey of triumphs over anti-Semitism in our culture and the sorry fact of an unresolved religious problem between Christians and Jews without emphasizing that another practical moral issue confronts us in dealing with the "Negro revolution." The problem of recognizing the human dignity of the Negro minority cannot be met adequately by either the Jewish minority or the white Christian majority acting alone. The common moral and social attitudes of both religious groups must result in a complete religio-political partnership. In short, the abolition of religious misunderstandings is a necessary precondition of an existential partnership between Jews and Christians in a pressing problem of our American culture.

The Talmud and Ecumenism

Whoever hateth any man hateth Him who spoke and the world came into existence.

Sifre Zutah 18

He who publicly humiliates his neighbor is, as it were, guilty of murder.

Baba M'tzia 58b

What a child says on the street, the parents have said at home.

Sukkah 56b

One man was created the common ancestor of all so that the various families of men should not contend with one another.

Sanhedrin 38a

A Beginning

Joseph B. Lichten

Sometime ago, Pope Paul VI, speaking to a visitor on the subject of ecumenism, recounted the following experience:

> One day . . . a Waldensian came to see us, together with a group of Protestant observers. He appeared at the door, walked toward us and, stretching out his hand, exclaimed: "Good day. We have not seen each other for five hundred years."

Today, members of the Catholic and Jewish communities are beginning to speak with each other, and we could very well repeat the Waldensian's greeting to the Pope, but with one significant change: "Good day. We have not seen each other for *three times* five hundred years."

Fifteen years ago, our continuous convocations of today would have been an impossibility. Prior to the 1950's, our communities were interested in each other; we talked *about* each other, but rarely did we talk *to* each other.

The first half-decade of the 1960's has perhaps witnessed the most vital surge of communication between us during the entire Judeo-Christian era. Our contacts have grown in depth and breadth, in kind as well as in quality.

There is a growing awareness that the urgent need facing our communities is education—an education which will eradicate distorted images from the thinking of Christians and Jews. A mass of wrong interpretations lies waiting for correction. Much of ignored history lies waiting to be learned. Not many Catholics understand the weight of the centuries of suffering which burden Jewish believers, since Christian-

Jewish relations are shunned both in catechetical and in Biblical instructions, and even more so in Church history.

In light of our ignored history and of the contemporary needs of today's encounter, we are encouraged by a unique series of pamphlets—published under the auspices of the John XXIII Center of Fordham University, aimed at Catholic parishioners across the country and designed to attack "the evil of anti-Semitism as a thought as well as an act." Called the "Spiritual Heritage Series," these pamphlets represent an earnest and dramatic attempt to implement the Vatican Declaration of Non-Christian Religions as it applies to Jews. They discuss the spiritual bonds between Jews and Christians; the deicide charge; the persecution of Jews by "the ancient church," through the Middle Ages and into modern times. They condemn anti-Semitism as "many times a sin," and urge Catholics to engage in "brotherly dialogue" with Jews in order "to learn about one another as human beings."

Bearing the imprimatur of Bishop Russell J. McVinney, with Reverend Edward Flannery, member of the U. S. Bishops' Secretariat for Catholic-Jewish Relations and author of *The Anguish of the Jews*, as editorial director, the "Spiritual Heritage Series" has a first printing of 250,000 sets. The John XXIII Center of Fordham University has asked American bishops to endorse the project and to urge priests and educators in their dioceses to distribute the pamphlets to their parishioners.

Published by the Olive Tree Press, a new publishing house formed by the John XXIII Center, the individual pamphlets are entitled: *Our Spiritual Heritage, The Outline of Truth, The Anguish of a People, The Face of Sin, To Talk Together,* and *The Declaration on Non-Christian Religions.*

Our Spiritual Heritage

Pointing out that "To the Jewish people, God spoke: 'You shall be My people and I will be your God,'" the pamphlet asserts that this promise gave the Israelites "a special place in the history of man." The first pamphlet states: "the gifts and call of God are without repentance" (Romans 11:29), and "the Jewish and Christian peoples have a fundamental relation in their mutual faiths and should exist peacefully side by side."

The Outline of Truth

The Outline of Truth deals with the death of Jesus and the charge of deicide "which for nearly 2,000 years has been a source of so much hate, bloodshed and violence directed against the Jewish people." It describes "the outline of this terrible event" as having been "distorted and twisted for all these centuries through misunderstanding, misinterpretation and plain lack of knowledge."

Urging Catholics to "sweep aside old wrongs and mistrust, worn half-truths and misconceptions," the pamphlet says the blame for the death of Christ "belongs not to the Jews but to the sins of all men everywhere. . . . He came in love and died in forgiveness."

The Anguish of a People

The Anguish of a People details the "page torn out of our history books" in order to make Catholics aware of "the depth and extent of persecution suffered by the Jewish people down the ages." "Without this page," the pamphlet declares, "we cannot really understand why Vatican Council made its statement on the Jews."

It goes on to enumerate attacks on synagogues, severe restrictions on Jewish life, confiscation of Jewish property and the killing of Jews through the centuries and up to modern times when "the Jew was subject to innumerable further pogroms and attacks." Citing the propaganda of the Hitler regime as having tried "to twist Biblical and Scriptural references to fit their own un-Christian aims," the pamphlet states: "These are the things you must know in order to properly understand what the Church cries out against today. She wants no more confused Christians, no more misled followers, no more Christians who fail to understand Christianity."

The Face of Sin

The Face of Sin likens anti-Semitism to "a terrible shadow of mistruth, misunderstanding and ignorance" hanging over the lives of two families.

"Finally, a time comes to remove the shadow, to open up a new chapter of friendship, respect and understanding. Such a time is here."

The pamphlet goes on to call anti-Semitism "many times a sin . . . a direct violation of the supreme Christian law: love thy neighbor . . . a sin against justice . . . a sin of hate and anger, a sin against the 5th commandment."

It further points out that "some believe anti-Semitism to be an unconscious or secret hatred of Christ" and explains the phenomenon this way:

"He told us to love one another, knowing it would take an effort on our part; He gave us codes of living, ethics, principles, restrictions . . . all things which require discipline and effort. It is therefore believed that many of us secretly resent Christ for this but, as we cannot face this fact, we direct our resentment elsewhere . . . against those from whom Jesus came."

To Talk Together

The fifth pamphlet in the series, *To Talk Together,* urges dialogue with Jewish neighbors and co-workers as well as taking part in formal Catholic-Jewish dialogues. "Be aware," it advises, "of all things which are being done to erase bitterness and misunderstanding between people. But most of all, reach out to your Jewish neighbor in attitude as well as in action."

"All the great decrees, all the beautiful words, all the fine discussions of learned men, will mean precious little," the pamphlet concludes, "unless they find an echo in your hearts, your words, your deeds."

The Declaration

The sixth pamphlet examines the meaning of the Declaration on Non-Christian Religions and its potential impact on Catholic-Jewish relations. In calling anti-Semitism "un-Christian—foreign to, against all that Christ preached, taught and brought to the world," it makes clear that "the Church attacks the evil of anti-Semitism as a thought as well as an act."

The pamphlet describes the Declaration as being "so profound that it is not just a statement but a deed, an act."

"And now it is for you, Catholic parishioners," the pamphlet concludes, "to make Her (the Church's) deed into a living reality in your daily life."

For you know the heart of the stranger, seeing you were strangers in the land of Egypt.

Exodus 23:9

What Is Required

Jay Kaufman

The Jew who supplements his preparation for a dialogue with Christians by a careful study of the articles in this issue of *Jewish Heritage* should be well aware of the mature level of Jewish knowledge expected of him. The days are gone when explaining the meaning and ceremonial objects of Hanukkah, Passover, Purim and the High Holy Days to a church group visiting the synagogue qualifies one for interfaith relationships. Gone too are the days when rabbis alone serve as surrogates for the Jewish people in encounters with the Christian community. Today we expect Jewish laymen, sitting alongside their rabbis, to enter into meaningful discussions with Christian neighbors who are likewise represented by clergy and laymen.

In our voluntary Jewish community there can be no authoritative monitoring of laymen, no insistence on proof of adequate knowledge, of bona fide credentials to represent the Jewish people properly in the give and take of dialogue. By virtue of their position or importance to the organization sponsoring any single dialogue, the ill-prepared can sometimes be jockeyed into participation. Sometimes the lack of high levels of Jewish knowledge among a group pressed into a dialogue situation may permit the knowing inclusion of laymen not yet qualified through study to participate.

The presence of inadequately prepared Jewish laymen purporting to speak as their people's representatives is spiritual fraud. It is a needless deception, for a Jew can learn his own heritage adequately. To permit his participation in dialogue prior to proper preparation is an act of irresponsibility perpetrated both by the individual and the sponsoring organization.

The dialogue is a delicate instrumentality designated to seek noble goals, but the dangers inherent in it are manifold and the damage wrought by those who misrepresent us, albeit innocently, can be a *hillul ha-Shem* (blasphemy).

Rules of Dialogue

The first rule of dialogue is that essential to that exchange is not what one Jew thinks but what Judaism teaches. Articulated is not an improvised interpretation of unfounded recollections but an authentic presentation of Jewish tradition. Even with sound knowledge of the Jewish past and value system, there are differing interpretations and evaluations in the application of Jewish ethics and theology to contemporary issues. Learned Jews differ greatly on the valid Jewish approach to basic social and economic problems. For much of what will be discussed in a dialogue, there are no set answers. But the answers Jews give, even though they may legitimately differ, must grow out of the seedbed of the Jewish past and positions.

A second necessity for participants in dialogue is a realistic expectation of what such exchange can and cannot achieve. For example, one of the goals commonly given as reason for the dialogue process is that it brings greater understanding of the Jew, and therefore less prejudice. This concept goes contrary to the basic principles of the civil libertarianism that undergirds American democracy and which came to this country from Biblical ethics by way of the Pilgrims and Founding Fathers. Nowhere in the catechism of our Republic is it implied that we have to understand the beliefs of a man in order to accord him the rights and privileges which the American Constitution and Bill of Rights accord to every citizen regardless of creed. The Bible insisted upon treating the stranger even as the home-born, whether his god was Baal, Astarte, Ra or some animistic fetish. Men are the children of the same Father and deserve to be looked upon as brothers regardless of their private beliefs.

The purpose of the dialogue is not therefore merely the understanding of one another's faiths but the pursuit of common goals, undertaken in concert for the good of our respective communities and societies. The dialogue falls far short of its potential if it serves only as an opportunity for an exchange of views on the theological aspects of each other's religious tradition. Only when it becomes the forum from which concerted action is planned for an attack on common ills will it reach its ultimate capability.

What Dialogue Cannot Do

Why then have the dialogue? Why not just plunge directly into common programs of neighborhood rehabilitation, the tutoring of potential school drop-outs by the respective youth groups acting in concert, bi-religious programming for prodding political leaders to undertake needed social legislation? Surely such action can be propelled without pausing for the extensive process of dialogue!

No, it cannot. There are stumbling blocks to cooperative endeavor, long-standing suspicions, century-old animuses, an ugly history of persecution which stand between people of good will and create a wall of separation between them, undermining mutual trust and cooperative enterprise. These the dialogue can breech and raze.

But let us not expect the impossible.

The dialogue can remove misunderstanding but will rarely bring understanding of one another's faith. It can bring light to misconceptions and rout century-old corruptions of the truth. It will not, however, make basic Jewish beliefs reasonable to the Christian or vice-versa.

The dialogue will not help the Jew understand why the Christian believes in a God-turned-man who was resurrected, in a Messiah already come to a world wherein the inhumanity of man to man accelerates with each century, in a vicarious atonement, through faith in Jesus, for sins which a man commits of his own free will, or that a man's beliefs rather than his deeds are the criteria for salvation. Nor will the Christian understand why the Jew rejects the belief in a Jewish "rabbi" from Palestine preaching what the Christian believes to be basic Judaism, or why the Jew has accepted eternal damnation in the after-life and the life of a pariah in this life rather than believe in the Son of his own God who came as a fulfillment of the prophecy of the Jewish Bible.

What Dialogue Can Do

What can and should come from the dialogue, however, is a deeper mutual understanding of one another by Christians and Jews after they accept the fact that the deeper they probe each other's convictions the more apparent becomes the irreconcilability of beliefs.

There can come, too, a comprehension of the "other side of the coin," how the Jew was forced into moneylending because all other means of earning a livelihood were denied and why for much the same reasons the Jew has gravitated to the self-employing professions in the modern age. Such new understanding on the part of Christians may replace age-old suspicions of sinister motivations, including a desire to dominate the economic arteries of the world. A new insight can be gained into the Jewish concern with the exposure of their children, suffering from the natural insecurities of the minority group in a powerful host society, to religion in the public schools, taught by well-meaning Christian teachers who count subtle conversationalist efforts a noble religious act—or who unwittingly think and speak of faith as synonymous with Christianity. Christians can also perceive why Jews have been supportive of the Negro effort for equality, how the Jewish moral imperatives on behalf of the underprivileged and the oppressed are buttressed by the ancient knowledge that one minority cannot be segregated for mistreatment without unraveling the fabric of the entire society.

There are the eternal theological problems facing the modern Jew and Christian alike: the purpose of life, the nature of the universe in an age when man is no longer earthbound, the universal hunger for the sanctions of a moral order, for an ethical code which in this day of dissolving standards parents can hold to and pass on in good conscience to their questing children. The variance in theological premises may be too great for a common search, but the journey together over part of the way can be mutually enriching and lead to the closeness that comes from sharing problems and seeking solutions in concert.

Rectifying the Past

Hanging over the dialogues is the gaunt spectre of the past. This generation of Jews lived through unspeakable Christian conduct during the Nazi era and came to regard the swastika as but the dark side of the Cross. Today's generation of Jewish dialoguers include those who lived through the days when rickety refugee ships escaped from Germany with their crammed cargo from the concentration camps. They saw those vessels, by the sheerest of miracles, reach the Holy Land only to be sent back to sink in the sea or to have their tortured passengers dumped behind barbed wire again. And all that while not a single door of any Christian country opened to receive them. No Jew can forget or forgive this infamy, but both he and the Christian will do well to ease their souls by speaking of it freely and without fear.

Hanging over the dialogues too is the mutual fear of attempted conversion, of a "hidden agenda." Jews must explain that the motivation for conversion is absent from Judaism, that our tradition holds that the righteous of all nations will find their place in the world-to-come even as the most righteous Jew. Judaism asks of the non-Jew only that he observe the Noahide laws of simple humanity, well covered in the religious demands of Christianity. Conversion to Judaism serves no purpose for the righteous Christian.

Perhaps the Christian too will re-examine his traditional preoccupation with converting the Jew and take to heart the counsel of Reinhold Niebuhr that his fellow Christians ". . . should remove Jews from the scope of Christian missionary activities, they should cease to support traditional 'missions to the Jews'" (see page 102).

Dialogue will not bring the Messiah, neither the first coming nor the second coming for which Jews and Christians patiently wait in this era. But it can enable Jews the better to labor *l'takayn olom b'malchut Shaddai*, to improve the world in accord with God's formula for the life of man on earth. And since, as Maimonides instructed us, Christians, like Moslems, as God-believers, are our legitimate partners in that task, we will move the more swiftly and effectively in its pursuit because of the dialogue's removal of barriers between us. Hopefully, it may propel us jointly to serve our common Father more properly as fellow men.

The righteous of all faiths have a share in the world to come.
Moses Maimonides

For let all the peoples walk each one in the name of its god,
But we will walk in the name of the Lord our God for ever and ever.

Micah 4:5

About the
Contributors

Rev. Walter M. Abbott, S.J., is Assistant to Cardinal Bea (President of the Vatican Secretariat for Promoting Christian Unity) and editor of *The Documents of Vatican II*.

Rabbi Solomon S. Bernards is National Director of Interreligious Cooperation, Anti-Defamation League of B'nai B'rith.

Pastor Poul Borchsenius of Randers, Denmark, B'nai B'rith Visiting Lecturer in 1964, is the author of several volumes on the Jewish people and on Judaism.

Professor Martin A. Cohen teaches Jewish history at HUC-JIR, New York, and is the author of a forthcoming one-volume history of the Jewish experience.

Rabbi Arthur Gilbert is Director, National Department of Interreligious Curriculum Research, ADL, and author most recently of *A Jew in Christian America*.

Rabbi Robert Gordis of Temple Beth-El, Rockaway Park, N. Y., is Seminary Professor of Bible, Jewish Theological Seminary, and author most recently of *Judaism in a Christian World*.

Rabbi Oscar Groner is Assistant National Director, B'nai B'rith Hillel Foundations.

Professor Abraham J. Heschel teaches ethics and mysticism at the Jewish Theological Seminary and is the author most recently of *The Insecurity of Freedom*.

Rabbi Walter Jacob of Rodef Shalom Congregation, Pittsburgh, is the author of a forthcoming volume on the Jewish-Christian dialogue.

Rabbi Jay Kaufman is Executive Vice President, B'nai B'rith, and formerly Vice President of the Union of American Hebrew Congregations.

Dr. Joseph L. Lichten is National Director, Department of Intercultural Affairs, ADL.

Rabbi Israel Mowshowitz of Hillcrest Jewish Center, N. Y., is Co-Chairman, Interreligious Cooperation Committee, ADL.

Dr. Reinhold Niebuhr is Vice-President and Charles A. Briggs Graduate Professor Emeritus, Union Theological Seminary, and author most recently of *Man's Nature and His Communities*.

Rabbi David Polish of Beth Emet Free Synagogue, Evanston, Illinois, is author most recently of *The Higher Freedom*.

Professor Ellis Rivkin teaches Jewish history at HUC-JIR, Cincinnati, and is author of *Leon da Modena and the Kol Sakhal*.

Professor Seymour Siegel teaches theology at Jewish Theological Seminary and is co-author of *The Jewish Dietary Laws*.

Rabbi Milton Steinberg was the author of *Basic Judaism, The Making of the Modern Jew, A Believing Jew* and *As a Driven Leaf*.

A List of Readings

SOLOMON S. BERNARDS

ORIGINS AND DIFFERENCES

*CATHOLICISM edited by G. Brantl (Braziller, N. Y., 1961).
Religious, moral, intellectual and social values of Catholicism.

*FROM JESUS TO PAUL by Joseph Klausner (Macmillan, N. Y., 1943; Beacon Press, Boston, 1960).
Common grounds of Judaism and Christianity and the issues which divide them.

*JUDAISM edited by A. Hertzberg (Braziller, N. Y., 1961).
Basic values of Judaism, under the categories of Jewish People, God, Torah, Land and Doctrine.

*JUDAISM AND CHRISTIANITY by Leo Baeck (Jewish Publication Society, Philadelphia, 1958; Meridian, N. Y., 1961).
Five scholarly essays by the late leader of German Jewry, including "The Faith of Paul" and "The Gospel as a Document of the History of the Jewish Faith."

JUDAISM AND THE CHRISTIAN PREDICAMENT by Ben Zion Bokser (Knopf, N. Y., 1967).
Subtitle is: A Historical and Critical Study of the Common Origins as Well as the Crucial, Non-Negotiable Differences.

JUDAISM IN A CHRISTIAN WORLD by Robert Gordis (McGraw-Hill, N. Y., 1966).
A history of the past and an outline for the future.

*PROTESTANTISM edited by J. L. Dunstan (Braziller, N. Y., 1961).
Varying interpretations of the mainstreams of Protestant thought.

*TWO TYPES OF FAITH: The Interpretation of Judaism and Christianity by Martin Buber (Harper & Row, N. Y., 1961).
Study of the differences and similarities of the two faiths.

CONFLICT AND TRAGEDY

THE CHRISTIAN JEWISH ARGUMENT: A History of Theologies in Conflict by H. J. Schoeps (Holt, Rinehart & Winston, 1963).
Theological controversies of the two faiths down through the present day.

EXCLUSIVENESS AND TOLERANCE: Studies in Jewish-Gentile Relations in Medieval and Modern Times by Jacob Katz (Oxford, N. Y., 1961).

> Changing attitudes of European Ashkenazic Jewry toward their Christian environment from the Middle Ages to the 18th century.

CURRENT STUDIES OF ANTI-SEMITISM

CHRISTIAN BELIEFS AND ANTI-SEMITISM by C. Y. Glock and R. Stark (Harper & Row, N. Y., 1966).

> In-depth analysis of the ways in which certain Christian teachings about Jews lead to anti-Semitic attitudes and behavior among Americans.

DIALOGUE AND PERSPECTIVE

A BIBLIOGRAPHY ON JUDAISM AND JEWISH-CHRISTIAN RELATIONS edited by M. Celnik and I. Celnik, Anti-Defamation League of B'nai B'rith, N. Y., 1965.

> Annotated listing of over 300 works on Jewish faith and life, and on all aspects of the Jewish-Christian encounter, past and contemporary.

THE CHURCH AND THE JEWISH PEOPLE edited by G. Hedenquist (Edinburgh House Press, World Council of Churches, N. Y., 1954).

> Christian theologians discuss the contemporary church's stance toward the Jewish people, and several Jewish scholars respond.

THE JEWS: A Christian View by F. W. Foerster (Farrar, Straus & Giroux, N. Y., 1962).

> A German Lutheran scholar's examination of the historical and contemporary presence of the Jewish people.

JUDAISM IN THE CHRISTIAN SEMINARY CURRICULUM edited by B. Long (Loyola U. Press, Chicago, 1966).

> Roman Catholic, Protestant and Jewish theologians probe the extent and nature of present and future Christian seminary concern with Judaism, the Jewish people and anti-Semitism.

TORAH AND GOSPEL: Jewish and Catholic Theology in Dialogue edited by P. Scharper (Sheed and Ward, N. Y., 1966).

> The first book to present primarily theological discussions of American Jewish and Catholic theologians and scholars.

*Available in paperback

Index